Praise for Ming Chew

"When I first met Ming Chew, I knew he would fix my bad back when no one else could. What I know now is that he is clearly the future of sports training and sports therapy in this country. If you don't believe me, just ask the New Jersey Nets, whose season he saved a few years ago."

—Mike Lupica,
columnist, *New York Daily News*

"When I went to see Ming we thought my season was over. With the procedures Ming used I was able to play and help my team in our playoff run that season. I had never experienced the things he did with me, and I know they were cutting-edge techniques. He really helped me."

—Jason Kidd,
Dallas Mavericks

"Ming's treatment was definitely the best I have gotten in my career. I injured my right shoulder and knee, and within four sessions I dramatically improved in both areas. I am a believer."

—Tyronn Lue,
Atlanta Hawks

"I'm both witness to and beneficiary of a miracle."

—Lou Schuler,
fitness journalist, *Men's Health*

"This therapy that Ming offers should be made available for players in all sports. For all the money invested in us, there's surprisingly little concern about the welfare of our bodies. My injuries of the last two years—both knees, my left ankle, and terrible pain in my middle back—were fixed in two sessions. No lie! I'm pain-free!"

—Sebastian Telfair,
NBA basketball player

"I first came to Ming around the turn of the millennium with a case of advancing carpal tunnel syndrome and numbness extending up to my elbows. Ming sorted me out in three visits. Now I see him a couple of times a year for a 'checkup,' and he keeps me straight, head to toe. He's always at the high end of the learning curve when it comes to new techniques. Go see Ming and feel good."

—Billy Squier,
singer/guitarist

"Ming Chew has been my friend and trainer for more than fifteen years. During that time he's helped to keep me injury-free. With an eye to the future, he leaves no stone unturned in his quest for new and innovative methods."

—Matt Dillon,
actor

"Ming's techniques are innovative and revolutionary. After years of immobility in my shoulder, Ming gave me full range of motion and renewed flexibility in only four sessions, which in turn helped me avoid surgery."

—Neil Smith,
general manager, *New York Rangers*

"Ming combines astonishing diagnostic abilities with vast clinical knowledge of how our anatomy works, plus remarkable skill. I had vertigo, nausea, and headaches for about two years and was beginning to bump into things. I saw three doctors, including two specialists. They couldn't help. But after two sessions with Ming, I was totally cured!"

—Alexandra Gersten-Vassilaros,
playwright, Pulitzer Prize finalist

"He really worked into me. It felt great. I'm feeling terrific. I'm definitely going to keep seeing him."

—Jason Giambi,
New York Yankees

"In three sessions with Ming, my pain is gone and my joints work well. With added sessions of strength building and Ming's stretching, my recovery is complete. Plus a once-a-year session for good measure. Everything feels perfect. As one friend says, you pay for your kids' education, housing, cars, and so on. It is also important to invest a bit in your personal health. Ming's methods are the best I have found out there. I have done yoga, massage, and acupuncture, and Ming's methods are more complete for maintenance and rehab."

—Jack Tilton, art dealer,
owner of Tilton Gallery, New York City

"Regular physical therapy felt like a Band-Aid. I always felt the real problem was still there. Due to Ming's treatment, combined with strengthening exercises, I was able to cancel scheduled hip surgery. I feel Ming's kind of therapy can greatly benefit all dancers. It all makes sense, since everything in the body is connected."

—Amanda Edge,
dancer, New York City Ballet

"To my friend Ming, the one with the magic hands: thanks for all the help on my injuries. Your number-one fan."

—Renzo Gracie, legendary Brazilian jujitsu black belt
and mixed martial arts champion

"When going to Ming Chew you can be assured that you are getting the most advanced treatments known to the therapy field today. He helps athletes get back onto the court in remarkable time. His personal interest in his patients also sets him apart. I am a believer. Ming's techniques are revolutionary, and that keeps my players on the court. When I need the newest groundbreaking therapy, I go to Ming."

—Rich Dalatri, assistant coach/
conditioning coordinator, New Jersey Nets

"After seeing a bunch of doctors and taking MRIs, my shoulder still hurt. I had severe, throbbing pain for more than a year. After two sessions with Ming, I'm pain-free! His techniques are unusual, for sure, but you can't argue with success!"

—Ed Faicco,
owner of Faicco's Pork Store,
Greenwich Village

THE
PERMANENT
PAIN CURE

THE
PERMANENT
PAIN CURE

The Breakthrough Way to Heal Your
Muscle and Joint Pain for Good

MING CHEW, PT

WITH STEPHANIE GOLDEN

New York   Chicago   San Francisco   Lisbon   London   Madrid   Mexico City
Milan   New Delhi   San Juan   Seoul   Singapore   Sydney   Toronto

Library of Congress Cataloging-in-Publication Data

Chew, Ming.
   The permanent pain cure : the breakthrough way to heal your muscle and joint
pain for good / Ming Chew with Stephanie Golden.
        p.   cm.
     Includes index.
     ISBN 0-07-149863-X (hardcover) — ISBN 0-07-162713-8 (paperback)
       1. Myalgia—Physical therapy.   2. Joints—Diseases—Physical
therapy.   3. Pain—Physical therapy.   I. Golden, Stephanie.   II. Title.

   RC925.5C483   2008
   616.7′4206—dc22   2007040355

3 4 5 6 7 8 9 10 11 12 13 14 15 16 17 18 19 20 21 22   DOC/DOC   0 9

ISBN   978-0-07-149863-0
MHID   0-07-149863-X

Interior photographs by Beth Bischoff
Interior illustrations by Betsy Kulak
Interior design by Think Design Group LLC

McGraw-Hill books are available at special quantity discounts to use as premiums and
sales promotions or for use in corporate training programs. To contact a representative,
please e-mail us at bulksales@mcgraw-hill.com.

The information contained in this book is intended to provide helpful and informative
material on the subject addressed. It is not intended to serve as a replacement for
professional medical advice. Any use of the information in this book is at the reader's
discretion. The author and publisher disclaim any and all liability arising directly or
indirectly from the use or application of any information contained in this book.

To my mom, who always stressed education and hard work. Although she came from humble beginnings in Hainan, China, she always led by example. She worked hard to make sure we had enough and instilled in me the notion of a work ethic, something I will always be grateful for. For these reasons and many others, I love you, Mom.

To William Goldman, a very generous man whom I've been working with for twenty years. Much more than a client or patient, he has become a father figure, and sometimes (as he would say) a rabbi. I cannot say enough to show my appreciation and love for everything he has done for me. It has been a wonderful two decades, and I hope for many more to come!

To Silvia, my honey and soul mate, who tirelessly supports me in difficult times and takes care of me on so many levels. If it wasn't for her, this book would not be possible. She keeps me in peak form with her wonderful meals and playful presence and, of course, her unconditional love. Thank you, Silvia, and I love you.

Contents

Foreword

I am, as I write this, seventy-five and feel better and stronger than at any other time in my life.

And why? Ming Chew.

We met twenty years ago. He had graduated from Columbia, gotten his physical therapy degree from NYU, was just beginning his endless trip into learning all the secrets of the body.

Me? I had this bad back. Had it for decades. (L4, if you're interested.) It attacked me in constant and unsurprising ways—I'd be getting dressed, tying my shoes, then that awful sound, which could mean my back had betrayed me again, which meant two weeks lying in bed, gathering strength.

Or from nowhere, a sneeze—two more helpless weeks lying there.

I remember once my family took a trip I was supposed to go on, couldn't, and when they came back, I was better and I met them at the door. My youngest, then maybe five, looked at me surprised and said these words: "What are you doing standing up?"

A chiropractor I knew thought Ming might somehow help me, so one day he came to my apartment. He is not your ordinary-looking guy—you probably have guessed he is Asian and you are correct—but he has also been a successful bodybuilder and his arms are *huge*.

So we met, and I described my problems. Then I said something that *terrified* him. I had dropped a pencil on the rug before he came, and I pointed down at it and said, "Would you mind picking that up?"

"No one's *that* helpless!" he must have thought.

"A girdle of strength," he said.

I had never heard that phrase. I wondered what language he was speaking.

"We'll just build a girdle of strength around your back. Take the pressure off your L4. Shouldn't be a problem."

Guess what we did? Over the next months, we did stretches and lifts that built a stupid girdle of strength around my back, and . . . and . . . and *I don't have back problems anymore.* I'd gone through a whole bunch of doctors, and this was the only thing that worked.

Amazing but true.

For these last twenty years we do all kinds of fun stuff—myofascial stretches at which I am way more helpless than you are—but they work, they do, and I can actually cross my legs now whenever I want to. And weight lifting and hamstring work. I won't bore you by going on.

Except to say this: I'm sure glad he picked up that pencil.

—William Goldman

Acknowledgments

Thanks to everyone who contributed to creating this book:

Deb Brody, for being so supportive and enthusiastic—an editor who is a pleasure to work with.

Beth Bischoff, for taking such great photos and making the process so painless and enjoyable!

Stephanie Golden, a super-smart lady and true professional who really knows her stuff—a seasoned and meticulous writer.

David Vigliano and Mike Harriot, my agents at Vigliano Associates, for representing me so effectively and getting such a great deal.

The models in the photographs: Tara Marie Segundo, M.A.; Paul Virtue; Jimmy Piesto; Mickey Cartin; and my honey, Silvia Ng, who offered their time and their bodies.

Johanna Bowman, for taking over seamlessly from Deb, and Susan Moore, for being so extremely helpful and making the production process so easy.

For various reasons, I thank Peter Gethers; Andy Miller; Rich Dalatri; Rachel Caplan and Equinox; Tony Hearns and Elysium Fitness; Mark Wood and Club H; Matt Dillon; Andrew Feldman, M.D.; Mike Ayala; and Renzo Gracie—they all know why.

Thanks to Joe Hayes, certified strength and conditioning specialist; Eric Serrano, M.D.; Nick Liatsos, PT; and Mauro DiPasquale, M.D., for helping keep my facts straight. All are tops in their fields, and I have great respect for them.

Thanks to Mike Lupica, who began it all with his article in the *Daily News*.

Great thanks to Michael Leahy, DC, for creating Active Release Techniques. And very special thanks to Guy Voyer, DO, a superb healer and teacher, whose approach to fascial therapy so greatly influenced my own work and who graciously gave me permission to present some of his stretches in this book.

Last, profound thanks to all the patients I've been privileged to work with. It was you who allowed me to hone my manual skills over the past decade so I can help others in the future.

PART 1

What You Should Know About the Fascia-Pain Connection

CHAPTER ONE

Introduction

The Body United by the Fascia

I n 2003, National Basketball Association (NBA) star Jason Kidd injured his left knee. For five months, the New Jersey Nets sent him to various specialists, who all failed to help. Kidd was facing knee surgery at the end of the season. Then his agent heard about me and the Ming Method. Willing to try even a weird alternative therapy if it could save him from the knife, Kidd came to my office, just before play-off time. After one treatment session, his knee was 70 percent improved. After a second session, his knee was fixed, and he was back on the court.

Before this treatment, Kidd had been afraid his season was over. But, he said later, "With the procedures Ming used I was able to play and help my team in our play-off run that season. I had never experienced the things he did with me, and I know they were cutting-edge techniques. He really helped me."

Kidd then sent me New York Yankees first baseman Jason Giambi, who told the *New York Times*, "My legs felt really dead, and when I came out of there, my legs felt good." And when I healed *Men's Health* writer Lou

Schuler's shoulder problem—which dated back to a high school injury twenty-six years before—he claimed he'd been "both witness to and beneficiary of a miracle."

So am I a miracle worker? Not really. My work is based solidly in science. But I routinely heal injuries, aches, and pains that most medical professionals believe can be fixed only by medication and surgery. I do this by treating a little-known tissue that's almost completely ignored in medical schools and physical therapy training: a type of connective tissue called the fascia, which envelops every muscle, nerve, and organ in the body.

In fact, the biggest difference between what I do and traditional orthopedic medicine and physical therapy is that they *don't* address the fascia. As a result, countless injuries that could be completely cured through releasing contraction and tightness in the fascia are treated incompletely with pain medication, muscle relaxants, and surgery.

Not just physicians and physical therapists, but many other professionals who work with the body know little about the fascia. Most traditional chiropractors, for example, don't address it at all, which in my opinion is a serious mistake. Adjusting a section of the spine without first loosening up the fascia is actually dangerous, because whenever there's an injury, the fascia adheres to itself and to other soft tissues, and administering a sudden twist can cause all these tissues to tear. More modern chiropractors do prepare the fascia before making adjustments, and in that case the treatment is likely to be safer and more effective.

Most massage therapists understand the importance of the fascia. But in order to make the kind of changes in the body structure that can really heal an injury, the fascia must be actively stretched, and in massage therapy the patient doesn't move. Though massage can help stretch the fascia, on its own massage has only a limited effect. I see it rather as a perfect adjunct to the program this book offers.

Alternative-therapy techniques, such as acupuncture and shiatsu, open up the energy flow in the body but don't address contraction and tightness of the fascia. I believe that these treatments would work better if the fascia were released beforehand.

Since most personal trainers are unfamiliar with the fascia and thus unaware of the major role it plays in movement, their clients miss out on the tremendous benefits of fully functioning fascia for both performance and injury prevention. And while yoga and Pilates training stretch the fascia, most instructors don't make this a focus of the practice. In any case, the work in yoga and Pilates generally is not detailed enough to address specific parts of the fascia, so there are many body problems that these disciplines can't resolve.

All these treatment modalities have value. But none create permanent change, since the fascia can be effectively healed only by stretching, proper nutrition, and being supplied with adequate water (hydration). Very few people have the skill of releasing the fascia specifically. It's an art form, so little known that it's almost uncharted territory.

But I was trained by the experts who created this art form. For twenty years, I've worked on all kinds of people and seen every soft-tissue injury known to humankind. I've successfully treated injuries whose causes ranged from weight lifting, jujitsu, and basketball to sitting long hours at a desk hunched over a computer—all through manipulating the fascia.

The work I did on Kidd and Giambi involved using my hands to release scar tissue in their fascia that prevented their muscles and nerves from functioning properly. But what I'll give you in this book is a self-therapy method that enables you to release your own fascia. You'll be doing the same program, minus the hands-on treatment. The Ming Method has seven components, all essential for maximal results:

1. Hydration: drinking enough water to fully hydrate the fascia
2. Anti-inflammation diet
3. Supplements to support fascial health
4. Spinal decompression stretches to separate the vertebrae, releasing pressure on compressed nerves so they can stimulate muscles to function fully
5. Fascial stretches to release individual contracted areas that cause pain
6. Strengthening exercises to make fascial releases permanent
7. Self-therapy techniques to do on yourself to facilitate stretching and strengthening

Using the individualized programs I provide in Chapter 9, you determine which stretches and self-therapy techniques you need for your particular problem. Then you can do them all in *only fifteen minutes a day.*

This self-help version of the Ming Method takes somewhat longer to produce results than if you were getting hands-on therapy, but it works for the great majority of injuries, even so-called serious problems such as a slipped disk and long-term problems that have resisted treatment for decades.

David's Self-Healing

It was David who first made me realize the Ming Method's potential as self-therapy. At thirty-eight, he was a highly successful real estate developer, lean and athletic, an avid jujitsu practitioner and kickboxer. Yet he had suffered from severe lower-back pain for ten years. Every day he lived with pain at a level of 4 to 7 on a scale of 10.

The pain prevented David from sleeping on his back. It increased with stress and when he intensified his workout. He was crazy to work out with that back, but being strong-minded, he persevered. He believed in that old chestnut "no pain, no gain," plus his martial arts trainer told him to train through the pain. So he medicated it with ibuprofen and iced his back every night. Meanwhile, he consulted three different doctors who diagnosed a bulging disk in his lower back and told him his only options were a pain-relieving prescription drug then and spinal surgery later in life when the pain got worse.

Then David heard about me from a colleague of his whom I had treated successfully. He showed up in my office despondent over the thought that back surgery lay in his future. In my eyes, he wasn't even close to that—he had at least ten options to try before even thinking about surgery. During his first session, I worked on him with my hands and then gave him a regimen to get his fascia in better shape. I instructed him to drink at least two quarts of filtered or bottled water a day. To decrease inflammation, he was to reduce his four to eight glasses of wine a week to two glasses and minimize his intake of sugars and foods containing trans-fatty acids (e.g., cookies, cakes, and fried food). Finally, I gave him a list of supplements to support joint health, reduce inflammation, and soften up scar tissue. You will be doing this same preparatory program, described in Part 2 of this book.

By his third session with me, David's fascia was ready for the Ming Method stretches. I gave him three spinal decompression stretches and six fascial stretches, targeting specific areas, to do once every day. He could do light weight training at 50 percent of his previous level, but no kickboxing or jujitsu.

At that point, business took David out of town, and he couldn't come in for two months. He just continued with the stretches. By the fifth week, he saw dramatic change; the pain that had been at level 4 was now at level 1. After eight weeks, he was pain free.

Once his pain was reduced to level 1, David was ready to begin strengthening exercises. Now that his fascia and associated muscles were released, they had to be trained to increase their mass (the extra bulk would act as a shock absorber) and to make them strong enough to maintain correct posture. Over the phone, I gave him an exercise to strengthen his lower back as well as his gluteus (buttock) muscles and upper hamstrings (back-of-thigh muscles), the major stabilizers of the back. I told him to do 2 sets of 12 reps, three times a week.

After two weeks, David noticed that his posture was more erect, and he could bound up stairs with ease and a new sense of well-being. Strengthening was the final component that locked in David's healing, because it enabled his muscles to hold the released fascia in place. From this point on, his pain was essentially gone. He sometimes experienced a ghostly feeling of his old pain, but it never reached even level 1. And he stayed pain free because he stuck to his program of water, anti-inflammatory diet, and supplementation along with stretching two or three times a week.

For me, the "aha" moment came about six weeks into David's program. While still out of town, he went skiing. He fell down hard in the ski run, and his back went into spasm. He called me in a panic: "You're not here to fix me, what do I do?" I told him to take a bath with Epsom salts and just keep doing the stretches. He did, and the next day he was fine. Before the Ming Method, he'd have been flat on his back, his trip ruined.

Some time later, I met Danny, a young trainer at my gym. Danny was an amateur boxer with a lot of fights under his belt, ready to turn pro. But he had chronic, incapacitating lower-back pain, severe enough that he couldn't train, even though he took large doses of prescription painkillers and anti-inflammatory drugs. A doctor had diagnosed a narrowing between two vertebrae at the base of his spine, which caused the pain by compressing nerves there. The doctor said Danny would need back surgery in a couple of years, threatening his dream of being a great fighter. I taught him four stretches and told him to drink a gallon of water a day and take fish oil, an anti-inflammatory supplement. I never laid a hand on him—but within two days, his back was 40 percent better. Two weeks later, his pain level was down to 2. Six weeks later, he was completely pain free and remained that way after six months. His career was saved.

David's and especially Danny's experiences showed me that the stretches could work on their own, without hands-on treatment, as long as the person kept up the hydration, diet, and supplementation along with them. It made sense, since the stretches create the same type of release that I perform manually. And you don't need a gym or equipment—they're with you wherever you go. So I decided to offer them to everyone.

Where did these magical stretches come from? They originally were created by Guy Voyer, a brilliant French osteopath, specifically to release the fascia. In my eyes, Dr. Voyer is the world's foremost expert on fascia. Some of the stretches in this book are his (offered to you with his kind permission), while the rest are my own invention, based on myofascial principles.

Origins of the Ming Method

The Ming Method has its roots in my own experiences. I was born and raised in Brooklyn, New York, the only Chinese-American boy in my neighborhood, and I was constantly getting picked on by other kids. Then in 1977, when I was fourteen, I saw a picture of Arnold Schwarzenegger in the book *Pumping Iron*, by Charles Gaines and George Butler, and it changed my life. I said to myself, "Wow, if I looked like that, I'd never get picked on again!"

Bruce Lee was also popular back then. He was Chinese-American too, and he fought people with his fists. So I thought, what better way to protect myself than to build up my muscles so people would fear me and I wouldn't have to fight them? I started to train. By the time I was sixteen, I had gained 40 pounds of muscle, and all the tormenting stopped. Suddenly I had new friends—the same guys who used to attack me—full of questions about training. And I never had to fight anyone.

I became a bodybuilder and won many titles, including Mr. Teenage New York, Mr. New York, and Mr. Empire State. I was ranked nationally and featured on magazine covers.

In 1984 I graduated from Columbia University with a chemistry degree. Initially I planned to go to medical school, but I realized that my passion was to work with my hands on people's bodies. Bodybuilding had given me a good understanding of how the human body worked. I was intrigued by the body and wanted to make it stronger and better. So I went to New York University Physical Therapy School and in 1987 began working as a conventional physical therapist. But all the time I knew in my core that something was missing.

In 1991 I retired from bodybuilding. My next idol was Renzo Gracie, a Brazilian jujitsu black belt and no-holds-barred fighter, and I started training under him in 1996. While trying to escape an arm bar (a submission hold) during a competition, I twisted my left shoulder and injured the rotator cuff so badly I thought it was irreparably damaged. I had standard physical therapy for it, but the results were terrible. My arm was so weak I could barely move it. I had pain in the front of my shoulder, I couldn't sleep on my side or lift weights without pain, and I was pretty depressed. I tried ultrasound, electric stimulation, ice packs, and ibuprofen—exactly what doctors recommended and what I advised my patients to do. But nothing worked. At the time, I didn't know any better.

Eight months after the injury, I visited a friend in Toronto. He introduced me to a chiropractor who said, "I can help your shoulder in a few sessions." Naturally, I laughed. I believed my doctor, who had said I needed surgery. But I let the chiropractor give me two twenty-minute treatments. In two days, the shoulder was significantly better—an improvement I hadn't been able to produce myself in all those months.

What the chiropractor did was treat my fascia using a method called Active Release Techniques (ART), which had been created in the mid-1980s by a Colorado chiropractor named Michael Leahy. ART is a form of myofascial release, a category of bodywork that targets the fascia. It dawned on me that myofascial release was the missing link I'd been seeking. It was a real epiphany: I saw that the worst thing that ever happened to me was actually the best thing that ever happened, because it opened my eyes to the benefits of myofascial therapy.

For the next ten years, I studied with Dr. Leahy and practitioners of other forms of myofascial therapy, and I still study it. I dropped ultrasound, electrical stimulation, ice, hot packs, and Thera-Band exercises in favor of myofascial release techniques targeting specific areas of the body. When I was doing just physical therapy and patients got better, I was never sure whether they improved because my work cured them or simply because time, rest, and nature did their own healing. But once I began practicing myofascial release, the changes were so dramatic, taking only one to four weeks and sometimes less than a single session, that I knew it was my work that was so effective. Over the years I've modified what I do to the point where it barely resembles what I was originally taught, but my work still follows the basic principle of releasing fascia. I'm confident that it can fix almost all injuries.

Discovering Dr. Voyer

How did I get from the hands-on techniques of ART to a set of stretches that anyone can do on their own?

During the year that followed my introduction to ART, I had a number of treatments from Dr. Leahy and other ART practitioners. My shoulder improved to 70 percent. It was quite functional, but it wasn't perfect, and I never stopped searching for an elusive something that would heal it completely.

Then the magic happened. Over the years, Guy Voyer's name kept popping up. I'd be at a gym and someone would ask, "Did you work with Dr. Voyer? He fixed one of my trainees whom no one else could fix." So I signed up for one of his seminars. Halfway through it, I knew I had found what I was looking for.

What really attracted me to him, however, wasn't all the stories of miraculous healing. Rather, I sensed he was a genuine healer, gifted with his hands. I was also impressed by his credentials as a sportsman. He's not only an osteopath and specialist in sports medicine and manual therapy but also a black belt in judo. To me, that's the mark of a true, well-rounded healer who can understand the body as no mere M.D. can. A degree is just a piece of paper saying you went to school, but a high level of athletic achievement combined with the degree signals a person who deeply understands the inner workings of the body. In fact, this is the model I aspire to. I've always wanted to blend many disciplines and come up with a wonderful technique, and Dr. Voyer embodies that ideal for me.

Learning the concepts of myofascial stretching completely transformed both me and my work. I used the stretches for my shoulder and experienced another jump in function and strength. The shoulder is now between 90 and 95 percent and does almost anything I want. It acts up periodically, so I do my stretches and it gets better. Remember, doctors told me that my shoulder was permanently damaged. So I'm pretty happy, but not happy enough: I'm still intensely focused on getting it to 100 percent.

I've added stretches of my own to my practice and modified many of the originals. All my patients now get a stretch program as homework, which has really boosted my cure rate. I tell everyone they are their own best therapist, not Ming Chew. A doctor's attitude is, "I will fix you with this surgery," but for me it's about empowering patients with the knowledge that they can cure themselves, even if I'm not around. I believe that if everyone followed my program of hydration, supplements, diet, stretches, and strengthening, half of the injuries that bring patients to see me would never happen. I also believe that the Ming Method can make 40 to 50 percent of orthopedic surgeries unnecessary. There's a huge void in orthopedic medicine right now, which this book intends to fill.

Are you aware that surgery itself is an injury? It creates scar tissue, which is exactly what my stretches mean to get rid of. Scars naturally contract toward their own center, pulling the surrounding tissues with them. If these tissues include a nerve or joint, the result is pain and restricted movement. That's one reason why surgery often fails to resolve pain and can even make it worse. Surgery should always be your *last* option.

The Ming Method Helps Everyone

Every lifestyle, ranging from high-level athlete to complete couch potato, has characteristic body problems that the Ming Method can relieve. Especially if you're a baby boomer beginning to feel creaky and restricted, or already have a painful knee, hip, shoulder, or back, my program will restore your youthful ease of movement.

As I explain in the next chapter, the fascia unites all the structures of the body. It's the one tissue that touches every single organ, nerve, joint, and blood vessel. That's why whatever your problem is—arthritis, worn cartilage in your knee, stiff neck—stretching the fascia helps. The fact that the fascia connects all the parts of the body explains why the stretches often focus on an area far from where you feel pain. Jason Kidd's knee hurt, his doctors diagnosed a knee problem, and his knee was what they treated. But I examined him and decided his problems were actually in his neck, right hip, and left lower back. So I treated those areas and hardly put my hands on his knee at all. He was skeptical, but that didn't last long, since the results spoke for themselves: within two weeks he was out there helping his team make the NBA play-offs.

If you look in Chapter 9 for the stretches you need to fix your problem, don't be surprised to find that they target body parts remote from the area that's bothering you. First read about the fascia in Chapter 2 and how the Ming Method works in Chapter 3; then give the stretches a try.

Protecting the Weekend Warrior

I've treated scores of weekend athletes. They sit in front of a computer all week; then on the weekend they want to play basketball. I tell them, "You expect not to get hurt? Of course, you'll get hurt!" All that sitting compresses the nerves running from the lower spine into the legs, reducing the ability of these nerves to stimulate the leg muscles. Since the leg muscles can't fully contract, the legs are weak. Then during the game the players jump around on those weak legs and wind up with lower-back or knee pain. I recommend doing the stretches on Friday night before playing on Saturday, and then again after the game to wipe the slate clean. If they follow this advice, they're fine.

Golf presents an excellent example of the vulnerability of the weekend warrior; this game poses great dangers to the body. Golf is a "fast-twitch" sport, meaning it uses powerful fast-twitch muscle fibers designed to contract rapidly during high-intensity activity. If you're moving fast, the chance of getting hurt increases exponentially. José Reyes stealing a base for the Mets goes from a dead standstill to an all-out explosive run; if his fascia is tight, he risks hamstring pulls and lower-back pain. Weekend warriors are much more vulnerable than professional athletes, because they're generally not in such good shape.

The average golfer is between forty and sixty years old, works in an office, is slightly out of shape, doesn't drink enough water, and eats sugar—factors that combine to produce tight, contracted fascia. This golfer is very likely to get hurt. Think about it: the golfer goes out on the course with tissue that can't move freely, doesn't warm up, and then swings a club that accelerates from 0 to 120 miles per hour in one second. The body explodes into action, twists the torso, and then must decelerate the club. If you play eighteen holes, that's a lot of swings.

Typically golfers develop neck, shoulder, elbow, hip, and lower-back problems. Lower-back problems in turn lead to knee and ankle problems. But I've found that three spinal-release stretches plus five fascial stretches keep most golfers playing without hurting themselves. If you've already had an injury, these same stretches will not only relieve your pain and enable you to keep playing, but also even improve performance: you'll have increased endurance and more precision.

Running is another problematic activity. It's a great form of exercise, but too often people do it with tissue that isn't prepared for the stresses that running puts on the body. Many runners have tight muscles deep inside the hip, which shorten their stride and cause their feet to flop out to the side. The calf and thigh muscles may be contracted, too. And often their feet are rigid, so each foot slaps down on the ground as a single unit, instead of bending flexibly. If you run on legs and feet like this (and often one side is tighter than the other, which means you're running imbalanced as well), you're setting yourself up for plantar fasciitis, ankle pain, inflamed Achilles tendon, and knee, lower-back, and hip pain. Runners really need to release their leg and hip muscles *before* doing any kind of serious running.

Women in particular should be alert to this issue. In my experience, many more women than men tend to overdo their cardio practices—not only running but also aerobics, step classes, treadmill, and dance classes—because they see these activities as effective calorie burners. But all that jumping up and down compresses the spine in the lower back, reducing the nerve signal to the legs. Jumping on weakened legs leads to the same consequences as running on them: pain in the lower back, hips, legs, and feet.

Even if you're flexible, you may still have tight areas in your fascia. No doubt you think of dancers as very flexible, and they are, but although dancers' joints move quite freely, there are pockets of restriction throughout their fascia. For example, dancers often have tight external rotators, muscles deep in the outer hip that turn the leg outward. If these muscles are not released, jumping and turning on them leads to injury.

Each type of athletic activity takes its characteristic toll on the body. (For the effects of some, see the sidebar.) But before you start rethinking your whole athletic life, just remember: no matter what injury your sport may cause, the stretches can prevent or fix it.

Keeping Yourself Safe at Work

Almost any occupation uses the same set of muscles over and over. Assembly-line workers are the obvious example, but I see repetitive stress injuries in people who do all sorts of work. An architect I treated was always bent over his drafting board. He had nerve pain from his neck to his drawing hand. Sculptors develop arm and neck problems, too, as well as back pain. Dentists work with the elbow lifted higher than the shoulder for long periods, so they also get neck problems. The same is true of hairdressers and makeup artists.

Even if your job keeps you tied to a desk, and your greatest exertion all week is going to the refrigerator to grab a beer, you're at risk for injury. With the advent of computers, occupational injuries among office workers surged. So-called carpal tunnel syndrome, which now causes more days away from work than any other disabling condition, has become a household word, but it's not the only injury the desk worker faces. When that person stands up, you're likely to see a permanently rounded upper

What Is My Sport Doing to My Body?

> Cyclists have shortened hip flexors (the muscles in the area where the thigh meets the torso that bend and raise the knee) and often tight necks.

> Jujitsu fighters have short hip flexors plus contracted abdominals.

> Kickboxers develop contractions in the muscles at the side of the buttocks, as well as lower-back pain.

> Tennis players are vulnerable to tennis elbow, shoulder injuries, and lower-back pain.

> Contact sports (e.g., wrestling, football, hockey, and basketball) are particularly destructive. They cause bruising when players crash into each other and cause overstretch injuries when they react to each other's moves. I've seen pockets of inflamed tissue and kinked fascia in every body part. Wrestlers who lift and throw opponents torque their backs and wind up with back pain.

> Yoga practitioners are often urged by overzealous instructors to push farther into the postures than is good for their body. If a stretch doesn't focus on specific tight areas, but instead stretches the body generally, the areas that are less tight get overstretched, while the restricted areas remain restricted. The disparity between them increases, so the body grows more imbalanced, not less. The result: over-stretch injuries. I see yoga practitioners with groin pulls, wrist strains, and hamstring pulls.

back, with a head that juts forward and a concave chest. What you can't see are the contracted muscles at the front and side of the neck, the shortened biceps (both factors in carpal tunnel syndrome), forearms chronically in spasm from typing, tight hip flexors, compressed nerves in the pelvis, and buttocks with impaired blood circulation. Did you know that when you sit on your butt all day, your gluteus muscles stop working? The glutes are not just something to sit on; they're major muscles that you need to stand erect, jump, and walk up stairs.

Put all these consequences of sitting at a computer together, and you've got lower-back pain, neck pain (usually on the side where you hold your mouse or phone), pain between your shoulder blades, migraines, a painful jaw (TMJ, or temporomandibular joint, syndrome), and, of course, numbness and tingling in the forearms and hands from carpal tunnel syndrome. Certainly, the office worker inhabits a very dangerous place. That's why you'll find my special office worker program in Chapter 9 that addresses *all* these issues at once. If you spend any significant time at a desk, you can't do without it. If you're not an office worker, but you sit for long periods doing anything else, you need it too.

If regular sitting is bad for the body, sitting on a plane is worse. Anyone who flies extensively for business needs the Ming Method. The dry air in the plane dehydrates you. Sitting for long periods in a confined space leads to lower-back, knee, and ankle problems. If you fall asleep, your head dangles, which shortens the front neck muscles, overstretches the back of the neck, and contracts the chest muscles. Fortunately, the spinal and fascial stretches reverse all this. The next time you come off a long, terrible flight, the minute you get into your hotel room, drink a quart of water, take some anti-inflammatory supplements, do four or five stretches, and take a shower. This will wipe the slate clean as though the plane flight never happened, and you'll feel invigorated. I tell all my business patients to do this, and they say it absolutely works.

Undoing the Effects of Excess Weight

If you're as much as 40 or 50 pounds overweight, your fascia likely is affected by the lifestyle factors that generally accompany extra weight: overeating, underexercising, and a diet high in sugar and trans-fatty acids (both of which promote inflammation) and low in anti-inflammatory food such as fish oil and raw green leafy vegetables. An overweight person's fascia also reacts to the extra weight by growing thick and inflexible. The combination of a large body, inflamed tissue, and thickened fascia equals little range of motion. Is there any reason why this person wouldn't get injured?

For you, my preparatory program is a must to reduce inflammation and hydrate your fascia. Then you can do the stretches to regain your strength and flexibility.

Strengthening for Elderly People

The spinal and fascial stretches can do wonders for elderly people. They're often reluctant to drink adequate amounts of water, and many take diuretics for high blood pressure. As a result, they're likely to be extremely dehydrated, and their fascia tends to be unhealthy. If they're not active, their muscles are weak and shrunken. Since plain old weakness is a big contributor to muscle aches and pains, older people really need stretching *and* strengthening.

Doing my stretching program—especially the spinal stretches—initiates a strengthening process that restores muscle function. Then strength training locks in those gains and improves on them. In fact, studies have shown that it's possible to increase muscle mass at any age. That's why I can't emphasize enough the importance of strength training for older people. And don't worry—anyone can do it!

Someone who's not used to active movement and has trouble getting around may feel overwhelmed at the thought of stretching, let alone lifting weights and doing push-ups. But I've designed both parts of the program to include very gentle levels that anyone can manage. Frail older people begin by doing easy versions of the spinal and fascial stretches while sitting in a chair. At first, they can hold for just a few seconds and increase the hold time as they gain strength. They can then do the strengthening exercises in a low-level, gentle way, as described in the instructions.

I've seen elderly people gain tremendous benefits from the Ming Method. They find they can walk and get up and down stairs more easily, their joint mobility increases dramatically, and they can negotiate in and out of cars and chairs without assistance. It all amounts to a huge boost in their quality of life. Plus, as I'll explain in Chapter 3, some evidence indicates that gaining muscle power can actually increase longevity.

The MRI Is Not the Last Word

As I said, I'm not a miracle worker, and the Ming Method won't magically repair tissue that is fractured, torn, or badly worn down. But I've found that you can't always tell how severe the damage is, even with an MRI. I've had patients whose MRI showed a torn muscle or ligament, and I healed them. I've had others whose MRI showed no problem at all, yet I couldn't heal them.

David's MRI

In treating David (whose story appears earlier in this chapter), I determined that his kickboxing was the cause of his back pain. But the actual problem wasn't in his back—it was in his right hip. Since David kicked more with his right leg, his right hip flexor (the muscle that raises the leg) was incredibly tight. Another muscle at the top of the right hip, whose function is to raise the hip, was also in severe spasm. Though the tightness was on the right side, it caused back pain on both sides.

It may seem peculiar that pain on one side can cause pain somewhere else—same side, both sides, or opposite side. But here's how I envision it. Take a pair of pants and lay them on a bed. Grab the right hip side of the pants, pull them, and twist them. The entire pair of pants gets pulled to the right, causing all sorts of distortions in the top and both pant legs. In the same way, a restriction in the right hip can give rise to all kinds of weird pains elsewhere in the body. It doesn't really matter where the pain is, because if you find where the restriction is and remove that, the pain will disappear.

David's doctors only looked at his lower back, and they diagnosed a bulging disk because that's what they saw on his MRI. His case demonstrates how MRIs can be misleading. An MRI will show the position of the disk, but it doesn't tell you the quality of the surrounding fascia. The doctors believed he needed surgery because they paid attention only to the disk, not the tight surrounding tissue on the right side. But when I released that tight fascia, I relieved the compression in his spine that was squeezing the disk and thereby relieved his pain.

I have no absolute proof that David's problem was not the bulging disk, though I suspect that even if it was bulging, it wasn't bulging enough to cause his pain. All I know is that after I treated the tight fascia in his hip, whatever problem he had stopped ailing him—and I've had this experience countless times. Trying the Ming Method before opting for drugs and surgery was certainly the right choice for David.

Bottom line: an MRI is not the last word on whether you need surgery, for its results are subject to human interpretation. I once treated a dancer whose MRI showed a torn ligament inside her hip joint. She had intense pain at the front of her right hip and was unable to jump. Her doctor told her the injury could only be treated surgically and had already scheduled the procedure when a friend convinced her to come see me. After some hands-on therapy, she did the stretches and strengthening exercises, and within three weeks she was virtually pain free. After another couple of weeks, she was back dancing full force and told me she'd never jumped higher.

I can tell you for certain that if that ligament really had been torn, she would not have been able to dance, Ming Method or no Ming Method. So I concluded that her surgeon did not interpret the MRI correctly. My conclusion is supported by a number of research studies reporting that diagnoses based on MRIs are indeed frequently incorrect. A surgeon and a radiologist often interpret an MRI differently, but since it's the surgeon who decides whether to perform the procedure, the surgeon's interpretation is the one that rules. A study published in 2006 in *Clinical Orthopaedics and Related Research*, for example, found that 37 percent of knee operations that had been performed after MRIs showed significant damage in the knee were actually unnecessary. In response to these results, Helene Pavlov, M.D., chairman of radiology at the Hospital for Special Surgery in New York City, said that orthopedic surgeons should not be the main interpreters of MRIs. Based on my own experience, I believe a patient should get a second opinion from a specialist radiologist (ideally, two second opinions) in addition to the orthopedic surgeon's opinion—and should give at least equal weight to the radiologist's opinion.

Reprioritize!

Once you begin the Ming Method, you'll know pretty soon whether it's effective for you. If it is, after about four weeks your body starts talking to you, giving you hints that things are improving. Perhaps you find yourself popping out of bed in the morning without the aches and pains you're used to. Maybe the peak intensity level and the frequency of your pain have diminished. When this happens, you know the program is working.

A great benefit of the Ming Method is that it can save you from unnecessary drugs and surgeries and their painful or dangerous side effects. People are so used to the medical model of healing that the minute something hurts, they run to the doctor. Patients with hip or knee problems have told me that their friends and family took for granted that they'd be getting a joint replacement and were actually disturbed when the patients explained that they were taking a very different path. With the Ming Method, you'll get a good idea of how damaged your tissue really is. You then can make an intelligent decision about whether to progress to drugs or surgery.

Therefore I urge you: lose your old assumptions and reorder your priorities! Instead of thinking "medicate and cut," start off with the Ming Method. Give it an honest try: do the entire program thoroughly for six weeks. If your problem isn't resolved or much improved, consult a practitioner of myofascial therapy (to find one, go to activerelease.com/providersearch.asp or guyvoyer.com/eng/index.htm). Once the therapist has done his or her best, see if you can get further improvement from strength training. The step after that is medication. Only as an absolute last resort, if nothing else has worked, should you begin to think about surgery.

You made a good investment when you picked up this book, because unless human physiology suddenly changes, the information here will last you forever. A lot of people protest to me: "I'm too tight (or too fat, or too old) to stretch!" And I respond: "Not true!" Because these are the people who *have* to stretch. No matter how tight or how old your tissue is, you can *always* create some improvement. The truth is, there's hope for everyone. It's *never* too late.

Imagine that you can tap a grapefruit with a wand and make all the juice disappear. What's left is the pulp and the flexible fibrous webbing that separates the sections. *Both* of these are the fascia. The webbing is like the fascia that separates one muscle from another. The pulp represents the fascia intertwined with muscle fibers and blood vessels. This means that, practically speaking, *muscle and fascia are one.* They look different under a microscope but are treated together. The term *myofascia,* as in "myofascial release," refers to both the muscle (*myo*) and its fascia as a single unit. This book uses the terms *muscle* and *fascia* interchangeably.

Fascia is composed mostly of water, two kinds of protein called collagen and elastin, and proteoglycans, which consist of protein and carbohydrates. Water makes up about 70 percent of fascia and muscle. Collagen, a very strong protein, constitutes about 30 percent of the body and provides much of its structural support. Elastin is structural and also elastic—it returns to its original shape after being stretched. Proteoglycans hold the water that keeps the fascia supple. (Glucosamine and chondroitin, well known as joint supplements, are proteoglycans.) All these substances combined give us this wondrous thing called fascia.

If you don't have enough water in your tissues, adequate proteoglycans, or proper collagen and elastin formation, you can rest assured that your fascia won't be healthy. That's why my program emphasizes drinking enough water to fully hydrate the fascia and taking supplements to support the health of its two protein components.

Healthy fascia has a gel-like texture. Moist and slippery, it holds water like a sponge. The higher the water content, the more gelatinous it will be. Fascia is extremely flexible and can take an incredible amount of pulling or compression without being torn apart or crushed, which makes it a great structural component of the body. Soft, hydrated, flexible fascia enables the body to move freely. For example, it lets a contracting muscle slide past the muscles next to it. Any form of manipulation, such as massage or stretching, makes the tissue more gelatinous and increases the fascia's mobility. So you can change the state of fascia by doing physical work on it.

Another key thing to understand about the fascia—and the source of the Ming Method's power—is that it forms a continuous sheet that extends in layers throughout the body. Think of it as a three-dimensional web weaving through all your tissues. Although scientific experts and researchers have divided the fascia up and given it different names in different parts of the body (e.g., plantar fascia, iliotibial band), fascia is really one tissue. This fact is essential to understanding its functions and especially what happens to your body when the fascia is injured.

Fascia's Many Functions

The fascia is a structural device—truly a universal tissue that ties everything together. It enables you to maintain correct posture, holds your organs in place, prevents muscles from tearing, and tethers muscle tendons to bone, giving the muscles the mechanical stability they need to contract forcefully. If fascia is torn, its muscle can't contract with any force. So you can't be strong and powerful unless your fascia is intact.

The fascia's firmness helps the blood flow through the veins back to the heart, preventing swollen legs and feet, phlebitis (inflamed veins in the legs), and possible blood clots. Tight, contracted fascia compresses the veins, diminishing the circulation of blood and also of lymph (the colorless fluid that bathes the tissues and carries white blood cells). Since one function of lymph is to carry off viruses and bacteria, poor lymph circulation weakens the body's ability to fight off infection.

The health of your fascia also directly impacts the condition of your bones. If your IT band is tight, for example, the main quadriceps muscle at the front of the thigh and the inner groin muscle at the back will be tight as well. Those tight muscles pull your kneecap upward, creating pressure on the lower end of your thighbone. Every time you bend your knee, the bottom of the thighbone grates against the inside of the kneecap, wearing down both bones. Eventually you'll have knee pain, but this pain does not involve just the knee—it's also related to those three tight fasciae above the knee. In fact, if you dig deep into any joint problem, there's almost always an underlying fascial problem that needs to be addressed.

How Fascia Is Injured

Imagine that I've put your upper arm in a magical machine like an airport scanner and you can look right through your skin at your biceps and its surrounding fascia. The fascia covers the muscle like an envelope and also sends strands of webbing through the body of the muscle. But instead of a smooth envelope and straight strands, you see little puckers—areas where the envelope is lumpy and the strands are shortened. Some spaces in the webbing are constricted, and the webbing itself forms little pockets or bumps, which are tiny contractions (kinks) in the fascia.

Because of the puckers, the strands of webbing have lost their full length, which means this kinked fascia is like a too-tight garment compressing the biceps so it can't fully contract. The result: a weak arm. The tight fascia also compresses the nerve in that area so it can't transmit a full-strength signal to the biceps. Eventually this nerve deficiency translates into more muscle weakness, joint pain, and possibly numbness, tingling, or pain down the arm.

If you do nothing to release the tight fascia, a downward spiral begins. The restrictions in the movement of the biceps lead to decreased circulation, since both blood and lymph require movement to flow properly through the tissues and carry off wastes. The body's response to this impaired circulation is inflammation, which is actually an attempt to get more circulation into the area to clear out the toxins. Think of your body as a beautiful, clean river, with a strong current washing the toxins away. When the current is weak or there's no current at all, the toxins remain in a stagnant pool, and you get a swamp instead of a river. Inflammation is the swamp—the result of a buildup of toxins.

Over time, in response to the inflammation, the body produces excess collagen in the form of scar tissue, also known as adhesions—more bumps and lumps where the fascia gets stuck to itself and to other tissues as if by glue. The adhesions create even greater restriction, increasing the imbalance between tight and looser muscles and causing further inflammation and swelling. The longer the inflammation is present, the worse it becomes, so you need to address it as soon as you can. Be aware: if you have any type of pain, you have inflammation in your fascia.

Causes of Kinked Fascia

Both overuse *and* underuse, as well as trauma such as bruising, wounds, and surgery, can cause kinks and adhesions in the fascia. Fascia stressed by overuse and trauma loses water, becomes rigid and stuck, and then clumps together with other layers of fascia or other tissues. You experience these kinks as knots in your shoulder or neck, for example.

Fascia can also become tight and weak when you don't exercise enough or from repetitive low-level movement such as typing, which is why you need a balance in your life between relaxation and exercise. The pressure required to type on a computer keyboard is low, and your fingers move only within a limited range. But if you type all day, the amount of movement is very high. The result of long-term repetition of small movements is, once again, weak and tight muscles, triggering the same downward spiral described earlier.

A third cause of tightness, kinks, and restrictions in the fascia is lifestyle habits such as bad posture. Think of an office worker hunched over a desk. Her hip flexors grow shorter during years of sitting, while her chest muscles contract. These tight hip and chest muscles pull her weight forward, creating stress and weakness in her lower back. The fascia in the lower back compensates for this weakness by growing thicker. Once thickened, it becomes shorter and relatively immobile. At the same time, the rest of the fascia on the back side of her body becomes overelongated and also immobile, setting this worker up for back, shoulder, and neck pain.

Last, everyone suffers the impact of gravity, which over the years pulls the spine downward, gradually compressing it. As you age, the effects of all these factors accumulate in your fascia. That's why older people are much more prone to injury.

Unlike obvious injuries, the small changes due to gravity, underuse, or lifestyle habits occur slowly and insidiously, so you don't realize anything is wrong until you find yourself with a symptom. It's like using an air conditioner for many months and suddenly realizing it's not doing much cooling. You take out the filter and discover that it's full of dust. The buildup of contracted fascia and scar tissue in the body is like the slow accumulation of dust in the air-conditioner filter. You develop small, silent problems all over the body, but because there are no symptoms, you're unaware of these problems. This is due to the body's many backup mechanisms that take over when the part that's supposed to perform an action fails. Once a symptom appears, you can be sure that these backup systems have been exhausted. That means you need to get the problem fixed, because no more compensatory mechanisms are left.

I Don't Care Where the Pain Is; I Care Where the Problem Is

Because fascia is continuous throughout the body, an injury to it in one spot affects other areas that seem quite remote. For instance, the origin of lower-back pain may be tight quads. When these front-of-thigh muscles are short, they pull on the hip flexors, which react by tightening and exerting a downward and forward pull on the spine.

All these connected muscles form what's called a *fascial chain:* an interconnected series of fasciae that are all involved in making a certain part of

More on Lower-Back Pain

Conventional medicine addresses lower-back pain by treating only the lower back itself. A doctor or physical therapist usually starts you with a hot pack, gives you ultrasound and electrostimulation (in which a machine delivers tiny electrical impulses to your lower back to release muscle spasm), and finally has you stretch your knees up to your chest.

But I've fixed many backs by treating first the psoas (the main muscle that flexes the hip) and then the middle muscle of the buttock (gluteus medius). One patient was very disconcerted by this. "Why are you touching my belly?" he exclaimed. "Are you some kind of pervert?" From his point of view, what other reason could I have for digging into his lower abdomen when he had come to me with a back problem? So I explained that people who sit a lot, as he did, often had shortened hip flexor muscles that pulled on the lower back. As it turned out, once I released his psoas, his back pain disappeared.

the body function properly. One fascial chain runs from the bottom of the foot up the leg and back, wraps around the back of the head, and ends in the middle of the forehead. When this chain is involved in a knee problem, the problem is somewhere in that chain—not necessarily in the knee itself. Remember how I fixed Jason Kidd's knee by treating his neck, right hip, and left lower back? The lower back is part of this fascial chain, so releasing it helped heal the knee.

For this reason, I'm always more interested in the place that gives rise to the pain than the place where you feel it. Since doctors generally look just at the area that hurts, they miss the restriction that's actually causing the pain. But as far as I'm concerned it almost doesn't matter what your diagnosis is. You can say you have a slipped disk, a muscle strain, arthritis—it's all the same, because once you address that all-encompassing tissue, the fascia, most problems will disappear. When one man came to me with a shoulder problem, I started by working on his neck. Not only did his shoulder pain go away, but his migraine headaches did, too. And I gave one patient a big, welcome surprise when I worked on his psoas and wound up curing his chronic constipation.

With the Ming Method, back-pain sufferers will do a series of stretches that target the fascial chains related to the lower back. You won't need to know what specific piece in that chain is causing the problem.

Luckily, fascia is not only an elastic tissue, but also a plastic one; that is, it can be reshaped by the right kind of stretching. Plasticity is not the same as elasticity. When you stretch a plastic substance and hold it briefly, it remains stretched out when you let it go, whereas an elastic substance snaps back. It's the difference between taffy and a rubber band. If you pull taffy and hold it a minute, it stays stretched out instead of snapping back like a rubber band. The collagen in fascia gives it a taffylike quality: repeated stretching and holding actually remodels it.

In the next chapter, I explain exactly how the Ming Method uses the plasticity of fascia to elongate tight, contracted areas and relieve the pain they cause. With my program, you'll be your own therapist. Listen to your body, and you can fix a lot of its problems. The whole purpose of this book is to empower you to realize that you don't have to live with injury for the rest of your life.

Test Your Own Fascia

Here are two easy ways to find out what condition your own fascia is in. Do both, since the first tests the quality of your collagen and elastin, and the second tests whether you're adequately hydrated.

SNAP TEST

Put your palm flat on a table in front of you, with your fingers spread as wide as possible. With the thumb and index finger of the other hand, pinch up a fold of skin over the back of the flat hand. Pull it up, hold it for five seconds, and let it go. If it snaps back instantaneously, your fascia is high quality and youthful. If it takes longer than two seconds to re-form, either you're dehydrated or you're probably middle-aged or older.

The older you are, the longer the collagen and elastin take to re-form. I'm forty-five, and my skin takes half a second to snap back. My fascia is in good shape; in another forty-five-year-old, it might take two seconds. In an eighty-year-old, the pinched skin may still be in a ridge after five minutes.

To give yourself an idea of what healthy fascia feels like, do the test on people of different ages. You'll get a sense both of how fascia ages and also of how it can be younger than your age if you're in good shape. A fifty-five-year-old can have forty-year-old fascia.

This test gives only a *general* idea of the condition of your fascia. Finding healthy fascia on your hand doesn't necessarily mean it's healthy everywhere. If you're reading this book because you have pain, the painful part of your body probably has unhealthy fascia.

In any case, whatever result you get is not your destiny! Fascia quality can be improved by hydration, supplementation, stretching, and exercise. Even an elderly person can have good-quality fascia.

HYDRATION TEST

For this test you need a partner.

Lie flat on your stomach. Your partner uses the thumbs and index fingers of both hands to pinch up a fold of skin on either side of your back, about an inch away from the spine, at the level of the bottom of the rib cage. Your partner pulls the skin up and kneads it like dough using a pincer grip, rolling the skin between the fingers. This test is not about whether the skin can re-form quickly; it's about whether it can be pulled up and rolled. If your skin is hard to pull or to knead between the fingers, that's a sign of dehydration. You want the skin to feel more like that of a child than like a piece of leather.

Have your partner repeat this pulling and rolling three or four times at points about an inch apart, working down the lower back. Some areas will be suppler than others, but if your partner consistently cannot pull the skin away from the spine, it's an obvious sign that your tissue is dehydrated.

CHAPTER THREE

The Ming Method

No Excuses—It Will Work

I'm a personal trainer as well as a physical therapist, and when I look around a gym, I shake my head, because most people are doing their training in the wrong order. They're intensively strengthening their abs, pecs, or lats without having first properly prepared their tissue. How do I know? I can see the restrictions in the very muscles they're trying to get into shape.

Consider the dumbbell lifters. In a normal, healthy body, the arm raises the dumbbell while the shoulder stays put. But too often I see a dysfunctional pattern: instead of staying where it belongs, the shoulder rides up toward the ear. The shoulder and arm muscles are too weak to lift the dumbbell, so the upper back and neck muscles take over. But this is not a job that nature intended for the upper back and neck muscles to do. Eventually, they fatigue, causing neck pain and headaches.

The origin of this dysfunctional pattern is tight, contracted fascia compressing the nerves that stimulate the arm and shoulder muscles. The pattern demonstrates why you can't safely and effectively strengthen

Outline of the Ming Method

› **Preparation** (ten days, minimum): water, anti-inflammation diet, supplements
› **Stretching:** spinal stretches and fascial stretches, once every day until pain subsides and then three times a week for maintenance
› **Self-therapy myofascial release techniques:** use along with the stretches
› **Strengthening:** beginning when pain level is reduced to 1, twenty minutes three times a week for a month and then three times a week for maintenance

muscle unless your fascia is healthy. Doing arm raises when the nerves that supply the arm muscles aren't firing properly is like putting on a tie before a shirt—you're going about the job backward. You need to get those nerves working first; otherwise, you're setting yourself up for surefire injury.

If these people were my patients, I wouldn't let them near a gym before they were properly hydrated and taking supplements. Then before they laid a hand on a dumbbell, I'd have them stretch out their biceps, deltoids, and rotator cuff muscles and stretch their neck. After this preparation, the arm and shoulder muscles, which are supposed to be the focus of this workout, could actually function and do the lift.

When you follow the Ming Method, you put each component of healing and strengthening your muscles in its proper order: first, preparing your tissue with water, an anti-inflammation diet, and supplements; next, stretching; and only then, strengthening.

Preparation

The crucial first phase of the Ming Method is to get your tissue into the correct shape for stretching: well hydrated and not inflamed. For at least ten days, before doing any stretches, you drink plenty of water and follow an inflammation-reducing diet. The basis of this diet is to eliminate or reduce nonessential carbohydrates and eliminate all trans-fatty acids. This means no juices, cookies, cakes, or fried food. You also take anti-inflammatory supplements, especially fish oil and special enzymes that enter your bloodstream and travel to the fascia to break up scar tissue and adhesions. (See Chapter 4 for details, including acceptable substitutes for your normal sweets so you don't feel totally deprived.)

This preparatory program is not extra or optional. It's essential. If you're not adequately hydrated, or your fascia is inflamed, stretching will only create more pain. Besides, water, diet, and supplementation are responsible for at least 20 percent of the benefits of the Ming Method, so without them you reduce your odds for getting satisfactory results.

Before beginning the preparatory program, you will rate your pain level (see the pain scale in Chapter 5). This gives you a benchmark for measuring your progress. You'll see that the preparation alone, even without any stretching, brings significant benefits.

Stretching

In the Ming world, there are two types of stretches: spinal decompression stretches and fascial release stretches. In Chapters 6 and 7, you'll find complete instructions for six spinal stretches and twenty fascial stretches. But don't worry, you won't have to do all of them. Look up your problem in Chapter 9, and do only the stretches listed for that problem. For some problems, you'll find as many as twelve stretches, but I will tell you which ones to begin with and when to progress to the others. At any one time, you'll be doing no more than six, plus two minutes of warming up, all of which should take you only fifteen minutes.

I've said that the Ming Method is self-empowering. That's because it's diagnostic as well as therapeutic. It's designed for quick self-diagnosis: since each stretch focuses on a specific muscle, the stretches you find hardest to do indicate which muscles are tightest and need to be stretched most aggressively. As you continue stretching, you're also figuring out which stretches you don't need anymore, which to continue with, and which new ones to begin. When I started stretching, all my shoulder muscles were ridiculously tight. Now half of them have really good flexibility, some could use a little more work, and one is still abnormally tight. I no longer stretch the really flexible ones, and I've shifted my focus to the ones that are still restricted.

Along with the stretches, I'll provide some supplemental myofascial release techniques that you do on yourself (see Chapter 10). These simple measures either prepare your tissue for the stretches or enhance their effects.

The Principles of Stretching

The extraordinary effectiveness of these stretches derives from a couple of neurological and mechanical tricks that they play on your fascia.

The first trick is based on Sherrington's law, a well-known principle of physiology. It states that muscles work in pairs, such that when one muscle contracts, its opposite muscle receives a nerve signal to release. Think about stretching your chest muscles (pectorals). Most people do this by putting their forearm on a wall and twisting their torso away from the wall. The problem here is that the muscles opposite the chest—those of the back and the back of the shoulder—don't contract; they simply bunch up and squash together.

But if you *actively* contract those back muscles while *also* stretching the chest muscles, the chest muscles receive a nerve signal—a reflex reaction—telling them to let go. So in the Ming Method chest stretch, you strongly contract the back muscles at the same time that you stretch the pecs. This double action releases the chest muscles mechanically, by pulling on them, and also neurologically, by sending them a nerve signal to relax. This powerful technique "fools" the muscle into relaxing.

The chest muscle stretch makes use of a second trick as well: it's designed to create tension in the entire fascial chain that the pectoral belongs to. How does this work? Suppose I spread a beach towel out on the sand so it's perfectly smooth. Now I grab it at the center and pull upward. The towel puckers toward my hand, creating a big fold. When I let it go, the fold remains. This puckered cloth is like kinked fascia. If I try to smooth it out by pulling at the towel, it'll take forever, because the towel slides around, creating new folds. A better method is to hold down one end of the towel and pull the other end. In exactly the same way, when you're trying to smooth out a muscle, you can exert more leverage on it by holding down both ends of its chain so the whole chain is taut. Otherwise, everything slips around just like the towel does.

Thus the Ming Method has you stretch the entire fascial chain that the chest muscle is part of, which runs from the heel of the palm to the breastbone and down to the pubic bone (this is done by holding the head, hands, and feet in specific positions; see Figure 7-8 on page 128). Tethering both ends of this chain stretches the middle part: the pectoral. We also add certain actions (e.g., pressing the shoulder toward the ground and pushing the arm away from the body) that lock the pectoral in place and focus the stretch on it specifically.

Let's see how this technique works for another part of the body. How do *you* do a hamstring stretch? Most people just put their leg up on a bench and bend forward over it. Their torso is twisted, the foot flops loose, the knees are bent, and the back is rounded. They're not putting the fascial chain that the hamstrings belong to in tension, nor are they activating the opposite muscles (i.e., the quads at the front of the thigh) to trigger a nerve signal that relaxes the hamstrings.

The Ming Method hamstring stretch does all this. The three hamstring muscles are part of the fascial chain that runs from the toes up the calves and the back to the top of the head. So you start by putting that entire chain under tension. Then you deliberately tense your quads, causing Sherrington's law to kick in. The strong contraction of the quads triggers deep relaxation of the hamstrings. (See Figure 7-25 on page 158.) You'll find that this stretch feels fundamentally different from an ordinary hamstring stretch. One runner and soccer player told me that the hamstring stretch I showed him was far more intense and focused than the regular one he'd been taught.

A second principle underlying the stretches is called Davis's law. It says that soft tissue reshapes itself in the direction in which it's stretched. So continually stretching kinked fascia lengthens it permanently, and its function improves.

The Mind-Muscle Connection

As you may suspect by now, these stretches aren't easy. They require strong effort and a willingness to face discomfort at the beginning, until your body becomes familiar with them. But I can promise that if you stretch once a day for only a couple of weeks or so, what I call the mind-muscle connection will kick in, and you'll really begin to understand the stretches. It's like learning a dance step. Your body repeats what your mind tells it to do until the movement becomes ingrained and the body can do it without the mind's prompting.

Some people need more than two weeks to develop this connection. If you're older and nonathletic, you might need an extra week to get there. But eventually even the most physically uncoordinated people have an "aha" moment in which their body understands what to do so well that the stretch feels absolutely right and completely comfortable. Once you really get into these stretches, you'll understand everything I've been saying about the fascia. Your own experience will be your teacher, and you'll reap real rewards as your body starts to transform.

Why Stretch the Spine?

To understand why the stretches that decompress the spine are so important, and why they must be done before you begin the strengthening exercises, you need to know a bit about the structure of the spine.

The spine consists of a column of bones called vertebrae, which are stacked on top of each other. The spinal cord passes through an opening in the rear part of each vertebra. Between each two vertebrae sits a spongy disk that acts as a cushion, creating space for a nerve to branch off the spinal cord and pass out between the vertebrae. Each of these spinal nerves carries signals to a specific part of the body, controlling its activity. The illustration shows what parts of the body each section of the spine controls. The spinal stretches are based on these correspondences (see Figure 3-1).

A healthy spine has enough space between the vertebrae so there is no pressure on the disks or on the nerves. If there's too little space between the vertebrae, the disks (which consist partly of fascia) can't absorb enough water to be adequately hydrated and perform their cushioning job properly. They begin to degenerate, and pressure from the vertebrae above and below may cause one or more disks to protrude beyond its normal space. Then you have a bulging, herniated, or slipped disk, and if it presses into a nerve, the pain can be excruciating.

Most of us have lost some of the space between our vertebrae, due to injury, the stress of work or athletic activity, or years of sitting. The job of the spinal stretches is to restore that space. This is called decompressing the spine. Guy Voyer has done x-ray studies showing that stretching the spine at every one of its twenty-three spaces every day for at least six weeks can increase the space between each two ver-

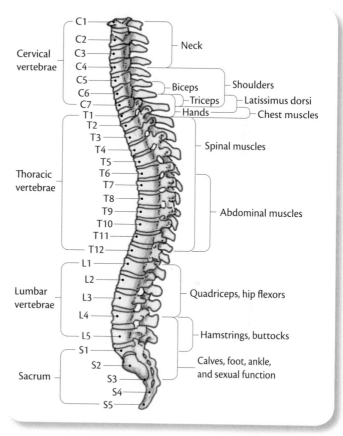

FIGURE 3-1

› Body parts controlled by different sections of the spine

tebrae by half a millimeter. That doesn't sound like much, but it's actually quite significant. A doctor may tell you that a compressed disk can't be fixed; however, by stretching the part of the spine where that disk is, you can create enough space between the vertebrae on either side of the disk to release the compression and relieve the pain.

Inadequate space between the vertebrae also affects the ability of the spinal nerves to communicate with the part of the body they're responsible for. It's like putting a heavy piece of furniture on your TV cable: it interferes with the signal, and the picture is distorted. This is exactly the problem with the dysfunctional dumbbell lifters described earlier. Compressed vertebrae in their necks constricted their spinal nerves, diminishing the nerve signal to the shoulder muscles and making them too weak to lift the dumbbell. In the same way, compression in the spine of the lower back reduces

Relieving Sciatica with the Ming Method

Sciatica is widespread in our society, due largely to our cultural habit of sitting for extended periods. Hours of sitting (even with good posture) shortens the main hip flexor muscle (psoas), pulling the lower back forward and down, decreasing the space between the lower-back vertebrae, and compressing the sciatic nerve, which begins in that part of the spine and runs down the leg. You feel pain that follows the course of this nerve: in the buttock, the back of the thigh, and sometimes down the calf. Sciatica may also result from a fascial restriction in the buttock or the back-of-thigh muscle (hamstring), compressing the same nerve lower down and causing similar symptoms. In either case, the way to treat it is to release the entire muscle chain from the lower back to the calf. (The program for doing this is in Chapter 9.)

the signal in the nerves that supply the legs, weakening the legs. When the lower-back stretches release that compression, the signal increases immediately. My patients are startled to discover that just six sessions of lower-spine stretches make their legs much stronger and more responsive to commands from the brain such as "lift" or "run." One patient found that riding her bike uphill suddenly became easier.

Like the fascial stretches, the spinal stretches take advantage of Sherrington's law and Davis's law. Suppose you're raising your arms above your head, as in the stretch called Holding a Small Globe, which releases an area in the mid-back (see page 98). Your upper back and shoulder muscles work strongly to hold the arms up and push them toward the ceiling. You are pulling the spine upward, creating space between vertebrae by releasing a set of small, powerful muscles that lie deep inside the spine and tend to pull it downward. As the shoulder and back muscles push the arms upward, Sherrington's law comes into play: the act of pushing up actually shuts off the downward action of the deep spine muscles, making the stretch even more effective. At the same time, this stretch reshapes those deep spinal muscles according to Davis's law, so they remain elongated.

Unfortunately, however, another law is also operating: gravity. Being vertical continually works against us, which means that countering spinal compression is a constant process. That's why everyone, not just those in pain, should make these spinal stretches an ongoing practice. If you're older than forty—the age at which the fascia starts to become dehydrated— you should do three of these stretches at least twice a week even if you have no symptoms (see my healthy person program in Chapter 9). They prevent you from slouching or developing a hump in your back as you get older, and they also maintain your ease of movement.

You may have noticed that even the relatively few elderly people who have quite upright posture walk in a gingerly manner, as though they find it hard to balance. While they may not have a slouch or curvature, their spines too are compressed. Lack of space between the vertebrae in their lower back diminishes the signal from the nerves in this area to the muscles of the legs and feet, and also to the buttocks and the muscles around the sides of the hips, which are important for balance. Because all those muscles are weak, these people can't walk normally. Imagine how strong a seventy-five-year-old man could be if you restored the space between his vertebrae so that his pelvis and leg muscles had full function again. What a difference that would make in his life!

People have asked me why the spinal stretches work better than the stretch from an inversion table, which holds a person upside down, using gravity to elongate the spine and increase the spaces between the vertebrae. First of all, the stretch from the table is nonspecific—it doesn't target the particular areas that are compressed. Second, the stretch that the table provides is not a complete release, because this stretch does not invoke Sherrington's law. Instead of releasing, the deep spinal muscles actually contract, as a protective mechanism to prevent overstretch. The stretches in this book, however, don't trigger this response; they induce total release.

The spinal stretches in my program target specific points in the spine where compression commonly causes pain in the corresponding parts of the body: the neck, the area in the upper back that forms a hump when you sit at a desk, the mid-back, and the lower back.

Stretching the Fascia

The fascial stretches focus on specific individual muscles that frequently become tight, compress nerves, and cause pain. Like the spinal stretches, the fascial stretches work by tethering the endpoints of a fascial chain. As

Fascia and Your Body's Global Positioning System

When contracted fascia compresses nerves, they lose a critical function: giving you accurate information about where your body is in space. Embedded in your muscles, tendons, and joints are nerve receptors that act like little global positioning system (GPS) computers. In response to your movements, these receptors send signals to your brain that tell you where each part of your body is at each moment. This ability to perceive your own movements and position is called *kinesthesia*.

Suppose we're playing basketball, and I throw the ball at you really fast. If your kinesthesia is off because your fascia is compressing a nerve, it's harder for you to catch the ball. And when you do and try for a basket, you undershoot or overshoot because you don't have accurate information about where your body is as you move and because the fine movements of your hand are impaired. The incredible precision of dancers and champion athletes comes from their highly trained nervous system, which modulates the speed, quality, and intensity of the muscle contractions that create their movements. If their fascia becomes unhealthy and weakens nerve signals, they lose that precision. I believe that if professional athletes and dancers received proper fascial therapy, they could easily extend their careers for five to ten years beyond what is now considered normal retirement.

Impaired kinesthesia also deprives joints and muscles of an essential form of protection. If I throw a ball wide and you reach for it, your kinesthetic sense tells your shoulder joint, "Don't extend that far, you'll tear!" But if those little computers in the joint don't work right, you wind up with a shoulder injury. Many, many injuries happen for this reason; I see them in NBA players all the time.

People often ask how I know when an athlete's fascia is damaged. It's easy: the athlete gets what I call noncontact injuries. For example, a basketball player goes up for a rebound and collapses in a heap when he comes down. No one was around him. His diagnosis is a torn ligament in his knee, which happened when he landed from the jump. From my perspective, that's a self-induced injury. If the nerves in his lower back were firing properly and his leg fascia was healthy, his GPS system would be working. The muscles that hold the knee in place would know when to contract and wouldn't put stress on the ligament. If he lands in an awkward way, those computers would protect his knee, and there'd be no injury.

explained earlier, the stretches are designed so that once you lock everything in place, you can zero in on individual muscles.

Let's look at the hamstring stretch again. It has three variations, one for each hamstring muscle. By doing all three, you can detect whether one of the three hamstrings is tighter than the others and adjust your stretching to isolate that one. This ability to focus on a single muscle is what makes the stretch so powerful. If you just stretch the three hamstrings indiscriminately, the tight one will remain tight while the others grow longer. The resulting increase in the disparity between them only makes your problem worse. You want to get the contracted muscle into balance with the others, and that's what the stretch does for you.

To get such a specific stretch, you must create tension in key parts of the fascial chain. This is why it's important to follow the instructions in Chapter 7 carefully, paying attention to the details of positioning your head, arms, hands, legs, and feet.

Strengthening

A nice side benefit of both spinal and fascial stretching is that they make you significantly stronger. But not strong enough: you also want a dynamic strengthening program involving movement. That's why the Ming Method includes a strengthening component to get you to the point where you not only function really well but feel vibrant and youthful in the bargain.

You'll begin the Ming Method strengthening exercises after doing the stretches long enough to reduce your pain to level 1. For most people, this means about a month of preparation and stretching combined. As I tell my patients, you *never* do strengthening while you still have significant pain. Pain is your friend, telling you something is wrong. Your fascia may still be too tight, and if you begin strengthening too soon, you'll hurt yourself even more.

Here's why. Suppose you have a group of muscles that are all intended to function together. But tight fascia interferes with the nerve signals to some of those muscles and also restricts their movement mechanically. If you do strength training with this restricted tissue, you're just training a dysfunctional pattern—actually making it stronger, imprinting it more into your body, and making your movement more and more unbalanced. That's what the dumbbell lifters were doing. In fact, I see this often in

Professional Athletes Deserve Better

If I were managing a professional ballplayer earning $18 million a year, I would never give him painkillers and muscle relaxants. That's a pretty shabby way of treating a star player, because it's the quickest way to retire him. Players take these drugs to mask the pain in a shoulder or knee so they can keep using it. What happens? The joint gets worn down to the bone. At that point, healing is impossible, and the player's only option is retirement.

Instead of simply relieving the symptoms, the smart thing to do is fix the problem at its source. In my opinion, these players deserve better than only symptom relief. I hope this book will start a revolution in how orthopedic medicine approaches not only professional athletes but also everyone else who makes a living through athletic performance.

I believe that my patients receive better care than most professional athletes. In fact, many of these athletes have come to see me privately, saying they wished their teams offered my kind of treatment. The standard treatments most teams provide are ice, electrical stimulation, ultrasound, painkillers, muscle relaxants, and surgery. Since their doctors are unfamiliar with fascial therapy, the players don't receive it. But if I were a ballplayer, I'd want it; if I were a team owner, I'd certainly want to give my players the most effective, least invasive treatment.

gyms, especially among people middle-aged and older: they lift weights with muscles and joints whose range of motion is restricted. This is simply crazy. The *last* thing a person wants is to make tight, contracted muscles more powerful. What these people need to do instead is get hydrated and then stretch to release the contracted tissue all over their body. Only then can they train with fully mobile muscles and joints.

For the same reason, I strongly advise against taking painkillers and muscle relaxants, drugs that remove spasms by preventing muscles from contracting. As I've said, pain is there for a reason. It's telling you not to move, so you can heal. Spasms tell you the same thing. Although a muscle relaxant makes you feel looser and better, spasms are nature's way of splinting the injured part to prevent further injury. So don't move it until you fix the problem. Painkillers and muscle relaxants may temporarily relieve pain, but they never really solve any muscle problem. All they do is take away nature's gifts of pain and spasm—protective mechanisms honed over millions of years of evolution. The dysfunctional pattern remains: you don't feel it, so you keep moving in the same unbalanced way. The result is pure disaster.

Why Strengthen?

Whether we like it or not, the human body is in a constant state of flux. At any point in your life, you're either getting stronger or getting weaker—period. As we age, our strength decreases. It's a very slow decline—each week you might lose just a quarter of a percent of your strength—but time passes, and eventually you're weak. This is why strengthening is most important for people who are badly out of condition. Weakness, pure and simple, is a primary reason for many of the pains and discomforts suffered by the elderly. It's essential to continuously, systematically stimulate the right muscle fibers to maintain your strength and muscle integrity and counter this weakening process to the utmost of your ability. A 2004 study published in the *Journal of Applied Physiology* found that men who had developed more power in their arms actually lived longer than others who had less power. It's not unreasonable to conclude from these results that strength training may actually increase longevity. While arm power is nice, the glutes, hip flexors, lower back, and quads are the true engine of good body function in daily life. Imagine building power and strength in those areas: you won't fall so easily, your lower back won't hurt, and you'll be able to pick up heavy bags and get where you want to go. Strong and healthy people are much happier and more joyous than those who are weak and full of aches and pains. All these factors lead to enhanced wellness, which is likely to promote a longer life.

Ask yourself right now: am I getting weaker or stronger? If you're training properly, you're getting stronger; if you don't train or you rest too much, you're definitely getting weaker. Pat Riley, the great basketball coach, once remarked that too much rest between games was bad for an athlete's performance, since the nervous system loses its finely honed edge. The average person doesn't need the strength and agility of a professional ballplayer, but the concept is the same. I believe that everyone should develop an excess of strength, so when the inevitable breakdown comes, it won't be so terrible. My own personal strength benchmark is being able to full squat 315 pounds (i.e., do a squat with this amount of weight on my shoulders) for 6 reps. As soon as I go below 6 reps, I know I'm getting weak, and I do something about it. Few people would choose to be this strong, but everyone needs to be strong enough to maintain a decent quality of life.

For all these reasons, the goal of my strength-training program is to make you really strong, and the optimal way is by using weights at high speeds—what's called ballistic training. In my philosophy, a stronger muscle is a better muscle. As I tell my patients: you can never be too beautiful, too rich, or too strong.

We do strength training with two specific goals:

1. To develop lean muscle mass to cushion and support joints
2. To strengthen stretched-out fascia, solidifying the gains achieved from stretching

Aside from moving a joint, muscles provide a cushion that supports it. For example, fully developed hamstrings and calf muscles are two pillows of flesh that function as shock absorbers and prevent the knee from bending too deeply. The first goal of strength training is to develop these cushions by increasing lean muscle mass. (Since muscle is mostly water, you also need to drink enough water to give you supple, fluid-filled muscle as opposed to tough, dried-out tissue.) However, just having supple muscles doesn't make you strong. You need to strengthen them to completely reverse the stringy, leathery quality of tight, contracted fascia.

It's tempting to start the strengthening exercises right away. Athletes don't like having to forgo their workouts for several weeks. But waiting to strengthen until after you've released compressed nerves with the spinal and fascial stretches will ultimately give you maximum function and performance. As we saw, when a nerve is compressed it's only firing at a partial percentage of its capacity. If you do strength training before releasing the compression, your muscles can't work at full force. Instead, imagine an ideal world where you have full nerve function, full muscular development, and optimal strength, working together to the max. Hold that image, and hold off on strengthening until your pain level is really down to 1.

The Ming Method Strengthening Program

My strengthening program has two phases. In the first phase, you spend about six weeks gaining lean muscle mass. (Frail or elderly people generally need about twelve weeks to develop this muscle.) During this time, your training focuses on a specific type of muscle fibers that respond to training by growing larger—type 2A fibers. If you are a woman, do not worry, you will not look like a female bodybuilder. You will simply be a stronger—and better-looking—version of yourself.

Once you've developed enough lean muscle, you begin to train a different set of muscle fibers—type 2B, or fast-twitch, fibers. These fibers give you what is called explosive strength. You need to train them because, oddly enough, they're the ones you need for ordinary daily activities. Think about it: nothing in the real world is slow, ever. Watch a person stepping off a bus. When she lands, she has to straighten her legs out quickly. Need to catch that bus? You run as fast as you can. Making the bed? You whip the sheet out to flatten it. Lifting a heavy bag to an overhead rack? A big, rapid heave. Even lifting a heavy pot from the stove requires strength, not endurance.

As I said, this program requires using weights. Even weak and frail people can use weights successfully, and they'll get much better results than if they don't. In Chapter 8, I give weights that are light enough for elderly or frail people to handle without injury but still provide enough challenge to produce real benefits.

In both phases of the program, you train for twenty minutes, three times a week, and once you've achieved your strengthening goals, three times a week for maintenance. A training session consists of three exercises, each including 3 sets of 5 to 20 reps, with a rest between each set. I've organized the routines so that each body part is trained once every fourth or fifth day.

You may be surprised to find that Chapter 8 provides only one strength-training program for everybody. (But I explain how frail or elderly people, or anyone who has never exercised, can start with gentle versions and progress very gradually.) People always ask me why I don't give them a strength-training program for their specific problem area, and I explain that they don't need one. My strengthening program is designed to take care of everyone's basic body problems, such as weak lower-back and gluteus muscles, or tight hamstrings, pecs, and biceps. Once you've completed the stretching program, your muscles will be released and balanced enough that you can confidently perform the strengthening routines without needing specialized attention to individual areas of your body.

My concept of how to increase strength is based on the Kaizen principle, a Japanese business-management concept that emphasizes continuous incremental improvement. Your goal in this program is to get a very small gain in every workout—a change that's imperceptible to everyone except yourself. In thirty days, you'll have made a huge difference. After sixty days, the previous you and the new you will be like night and day.

The Rest of Your Life

As I'll explain in Chapter 6, the best time to do the spinal stretches is just before going to bed at night. When my patients complain that they're too tired at that time to stretch, I say, "It matters little to me whether you go to sleep at 11:00 or 11:04. Just do the stretches!" Overall, doing both types of stretches takes up four to ten minutes out of a day. It takes fifteen seconds to drink 8 ounces of water and swallow a pill. With strengthening, we're talking about twenty minutes, three times a week at most. That's not much imposition on your life, but the payback will be huge. So do the program—no excuses!

Remember, though, that whatever your problem is now, it didn't happen overnight. For example, if you're an office worker, it probably took you twenty-five years to develop that Neanderthal posture. You can undo it with the Ming Method, but it will take some time and some effort. And as powerful as my program is, it will not give you permanent pain relief unless you keep your tissue healthy: hydrated, soft, flexible, and stretched out. You don't need to be rigid, but you must remain mindful of what your fascia needs. Once you're relatively symptom free, you can stretch just three times a week, and you can slack off on supplements a bit—though you do have to continue drinking generous amounts of water.

As I tell my patients, we're playing an odds game to improve your outcome. My philosophy is that when you have a problem, you should take many different measures to fix it: stretches, strengthening, self-therapy techniques, water, diet, and supplements. Even if each measure is quite small, they all add up, and over time the body is convinced it should be pain free. That's why the Ming Method can fix old injuries that seemed unfixable.

As people age, particularly during their sixties and seventies, their muscles begin to waste away and their lean body mass is replaced by nothing or by scar tissue. That's why so many older people are weak and stiff and their bodies have a stringy look. By contrast, the goal of the Ming Method is to leave you with a flexible body and full, supple, functional muscles that also look good.

Since we're all in a state of constant flux, down to the individual cells in our muscles, even a condition that seems permanent can always be improved, if not totally cured. Deep down, you know that the human organism does not want to be in pain. You weren't born with lower-back pain; as a child or teenager you likely were invincible, vital, and exuberant. That's the normal state of the organism, and the body has an innate intelligence that makes it want to return to that state. All you have to do is encourage it a bit—give it the right nutrients, water, and a bit of good self-therapy, and it will return to a pain-free state.

So remember: *pain-free is normal*. Pain is your friend, an indicator that you need to make changes, and the Ming Method is a map showing you how to chart the changes your particular body requires. I urge you to learn to read the signals your body sends you, start communicating with it, and become your own therapist.

PART 2

The Ming Method

CHAPTER FOUR

Prepare

Water, Diet, and Supplements

W hen Deborah called me, needing treatment for hip and lower-back pain, I was so busy I couldn't give her an appointment for ten days. So Deborah—a forty-four-year-old systems analyst and a very smart woman—asked, "Is there anything I can do right now that would make the treatment work better?" It was as if the ideal patient had descended from heaven. I said, "Absolutely!" and told her to start drinking water.

This was a new idea for Deborah, who had never consumed water by itself, only with food. I said, "Look at each pint of water as medicine, the cheapest medicine you'll ever use." I instructed her to drink a pint at least fifteen minutes before each meal, plus another pint over the course of the day. I also told her to take two tablespoons of fish oil a day. The fish oil was no problem, but Deborah claimed she already drank three to four cups of water a day, so she needed only two additional pints. However, I asked her to write down exactly how much water she drank, to make sure she took in two full quarts. When she did this, she discovered, as many of my patients do, that she actually drank much less than she thought—only a cup and a half. She was in a chronic state of dehydration.

Deborah was a triathlete who also spent a lot of time at her computer and never stretched much. She'd had hip and lower-back pain for about nine months and couldn't run. No doctor had been able to help her. Yet when she arrived for her appointment, she reported (to her own amazement, but not mine) that during the intervening ten days, her pain level had dropped from 5 to 3.

Deborah's experience is a perfect example of how powerful hydration and fish oil are as forms of treatment. And she isn't an isolated case. Whenever a new patient can't come to see me for a couple of weeks, I tell him or her to start on water and fish oil. Most of those who follow my advice have the same experience Deborah had. I wasn't joking when I told her that water is a medicine. Virtually every chemical reaction in the body occurs in a water environment. It simply makes sense to stay well hydrated to facilitate these reactions. I've seen dehydrated people with headaches drink a quart of water, and the headache disappears within an hour. When people with creaky joints and chronic constipation start drinking enough water, their conditions go away. If that's not the definition of medicine, what is? Water is a true cure, not a drug that only relieves symptoms.

This chapter urges you to make three key "medicinal" changes in your lifestyle that will lead to huge payoffs:

> Drink more water.
> Reduce sugar and trans-fatty acids in your diet.
> Take fish oil and fascia-supporting supplements.

Many think they can cheat on this part of the Ming Method. I admit, some of my recommendations amount to a pain in the neck. But remember that you're playing an odds game here, really trying to stack those odds in your favor. To make sure the stretches work for you to the max, you must complement them with proper hydration, an inflammation-reducing diet, and supplements that help your fascia stay healthy. You don't have to be totally rigid about it, but if you cheat in any major way, you're only cheating yourself.

Important: before beginning the preparatory program, use the pain scale and instructions in Chapter 5 to rate your pain level and write a paragraph describing your pain.

Hydrate, Hydrate! Why Water Is Essential

We all know that water is essential to life; every system in the body needs it to function. Depending on a person's age and amount of muscle, water makes up between 60 and 75 percent of the human body as a whole, 70 percent of the brain, and almost 90 percent of the lungs. As explained in Chapter 2, water is crucial for the fascia, which consists of about 70 percent water. It's also critical for a healthy spine, since the spinal disks are more than 70 percent water. (In babies, the disks are 95 percent water, which shows how much we dry up as we age.) When these disks aren't fully hydrated, they can't perform their function of cushioning the vertebrae and the spinal nerves. As people age, these disks dry out, so it becomes even more important to consciously replenish their water supply. (The bodies of elderly people who are dehydrated contain as little as 50 percent water.)

Whatever your age, *you must be hydrated* before you begin your stretching program! When fascia is dehydrated, it gets tight and inflamed and develops microtears. Trying to stretch inflamed fascia only creates more pain—plus, you'll deprive yourself of at least 20 percent of the Ming Method's potential benefit. So give yourself the two tests for healthy fascia in Chapter 2, and if they show that you're not adequately hydrated, spend ten days getting your fascia good and wet.

How Much Water Do You Need?

Experts offer a range of answers to this question, from "Drink only when thirsty," to "Drink enough to replace the fluids you lose through breathing, perspiration, and elimination," to "Drink the amount I recommend." For example, the Food and Nutrition Board of the Institute of Medicine recommends that women drink about 2.2 liters (nine 8-ounce glasses) of water a day, and men about 3 liters (thirteen 8-ounce glasses).

Here are my own guidelines, based on years of observation of myself, my patients, and people in gyms; on talking to doctors I respect; and on research. (One liter equals 1.06 quarts; so for all practical purposes, liters and quarts are interchangeable. If you're measuring in liters, you'll drink a very small amount more, which can only help.)

> Men less than 200 pounds: 2.5 quarts per day
> Men more than 200 pounds: 3 quarts per day
> Male athletes more than 200 pounds: at least 3.5 quarts per day
> Women less than 150 pounds: 2 quarts per day
> Women more than 150 pounds: 2.5 quarts per day
> Women athletes more than 150 pounds: 3 quarts per day

These amounts will make you well hydrated without your running any risk of drinking *too much* water, which can be a problem, too. Remember, though, that the preceding numbers are approximations. The amount of water you need changes from day to day based on how much you perspire, the water content of your food, the amount of alcohol you drink (alcohol is dehydrating), and your activity level (if you're exercising when it's hot out, you need more water). But the *minimum* amounts of water anyone should drink are as follows:

> Men of any age, in any condition: 2 quarts a day
> Women of any age, in any condition: 1.5 quarts a day

Many of my patients balk at this prescription. A common complaint is, "I'm not used to drinking this much water—I'm gagging on it!" An even bigger one is, "I have to get up at 4 A.M. to urinate!" And I respond, "So do I, but I do it anyway." People ask me why my skin looks so good and why I'm so healthy. The main reason is that I drink enough water, and peeing is a very small price to pay for that. As far as I'm concerned, it's no price at all. What price would you set on being healthy and pain free? Is it really such an imposition on your life to urinate a few extra times a day, considering the benefits? I call hydration and the other two key practices that this chapter recommends "lifestyle changes" because they do involve a certain level of adjustment. As I say to my patients, "Get used to it."

If you're like most people, you're dehydrated and don't even know it. After a long period of chronic dehydration, the body loses its ability to detect whether it's thirsty. So you need to deliberately drink more than you may *feel* you need. You'll find that as your body grows accustomed to taking in more water, your water-detection mechanism kicks back into gear and your desire for water actually increases. What may seem at the beginning like much too much to drink will become easy to swallow after as little as two weeks. In fact, it will feel normal and necessary. Expect your body to request more water as it becomes more hydrated. When it starts regulating water as it was intended to, you're truly well hydrated.

Getting hydrated brings a couple of nice bonuses. A big one is the change in your face. Your skin will look smoother and more youthful because of the water underneath. When I put Rick on hydration, he was fifty-four. After three weeks, his wife swore he looked ten years younger, and he did look fantastic. His skin was much softer and smoother; some of his wrinkles had smoothed out. Another great side effect of hydration for most people is an increased ability to lose weight. Research has shown that bringing more water into the body cells actually increases the rate of metabolism, thus helping burn calories.

Generally, it takes about six weeks to become fully hydrated. But I don't want to make you wait that long to get to the stretches, so I'm only asking you to do ten days of preparation. As you embark on your stretch program, you'll continue to hydrate, so by the end of six weeks of stretching, you'll have been drinking water for about eight weeks and should be fully hydrated.

To enhance the benefits of hydration, I suggest that you add trace minerals to your diet. The body needs tiny amounts of a variety of minerals, including chromium, vanadium, manganese, iron, copper, and zinc, to function properly. These minerals are the spark plugs of water, facilitating its chemical reactions. An excellent way to get these minerals is to use Celtic or Himalayan salt in your food instead of regular table salt. These types of salt retain naturally present minerals that have been refined out of table salt, which contains excessive sodium. The sodium content of Celtic and Himalayan salt (available in health food stores or online) is lower than that of table salt, so it's more suitable for people with high blood pressure. **Important:** if you have high blood pressure, consult a complementary-integrative medical doctor about using any form of salt.

A note for athletes: there's been a lot of publicity about a condition called hyponatremia. News stories have focused on runners who developed it after distance runs, when sweating combined with drinking large amounts of water diluted the amount of sodium in their blood. Symptoms include nausea, confusion, cramps, weakness, and in severe cases, coma or even death. Hyponatremia usually occurs when someone has exercised intensively for more than sixty minutes while consuming more than 1.5 quarts of water per hour.

Most people don't have to worry about hyponatremia at all, and athletes can easily avoid it by drinking 2 ounces every fifteen minutes while exercising and then drinking more when they finish their workout. Don't let concerns about overconsuming water interfere with following my extremely beneficial hydration program.

What Kind of Water?

I don't like municipal water. It's very impure, full of lead, fluoride, chlorine, and other unmentionable things. Lead causes a range of health problems in adults as well as children. Chlorine has been linked to heart disease, and fluoride is carcinogenic, damages collagen, and prevents certain enzymes from working (it's used in rat poison for this reason). Researchers have also found plastic residues in municipal water that many scientists suspect act as synthetic estrogens (xenoestrogens) in the human body, causing cancer and other medical problems.

So I recommend that you avoid drinking water straight from the tap. One alternative is bottled water. However, bottled water is expensive and generates a lot of plastic trash. For me, buying a good filter is the way to go. It's cheaper in the long run and kinder to the environment. If you don't want to spend a lot, at the very least use a charcoal-based filter system like Brita or Pur. That's better than nothing, although it doesn't take care of all the problems in the water. Fancier filters that remove more impurities are better. I use an Akai Ionizer Plus water purifier that filters chemicals and bacteria, treats the water with ultraviolet light, and ionizes it. The ionizing process is said to make the water and the minerals it contains easier for the body to absorb. The Akai is top-of-the-line and not cheap, but there are plenty of in-between options.

Whatever system you choose, store your filtered water in glass containers. There is evidence that any form of plastic eventually leaches chemicals into the water (even polycarbonate plastic, which previously was thought not to leach). If you need to carry bottled water around, you have to use plastic, but try not to drink water that has sat in the container for more than a few hours, especially at high temperatures.

How to Hydrate

Begin your hydration program by drinking an 8-ounce cup of water three times a day, before each meal. As soon as you can, drink 16 ounces before each meal. Most people can do this within a day or so. Once you're at that level, it won't be hard to add whatever additional amount your own body requires. Believe me, there's no physical limitation—there's only a *psychological* limitation. Think of pure filtered or bottled water as extremely therapeutic. Once you're in that mind-set, you'll drink it.

Drink your water on an empty stomach, because that's when it's most easily absorbed by your fascia. If you're drinking it before a meal, don't eat for at least fifteen minutes after the last sip, so the water goes directly into the fascia and doesn't interfere with digestion. After a meal, wait two hours before drinking more water, to allow for complete digestion.

During meals, it's preferable not to drink at all. Combining liquid with your food dilutes the stomach enzymes, which means you don't digest proteins properly—and you need those proteins for healthy fascia. If you drink the amount of water I recommend before your meal, you won't feel the need for a lot of liquid while you eat. Again, there's no need to be rigid. It's OK to drink a little water to help swallow your food or to take your fish oil afterward; those few ounces won't dilute the enzymes that much. If you like a cup of tea or coffee after a meal, go ahead.

Your Anti-Inflammation Diet

As Chapter 2 explained, improving the quality of your fascia requires clearing out the swamp of inflammation that's causing pain and building up scar tissue. Naturally, you want to avoid anything that undermines this healing process by feeding the inflammation. That's why you must do your best to eliminate, or at least substantially reduce, two highly destructive substances from your diet: sugar and trans-fatty acids. Both are powerful promoters of inflammation.

If your fascia is already inflamed—and let me tell you, if you have pain, it is—and you eat these pro-inflammatory foods, you will exacerbate that inflammation. It's like fanning the flames of a fire. I see many people eating sugar, fried foods, potato chips—and then they wonder why they're in pain. Your goal is to quell the inflammation, not add fuel to the fire.

Reduce Sugar

Notice I don't insist that you eliminate sugar totally. It would be great if you could, but I'm being realistic. Sugar is deeply embedded in our lives. It's everywhere, hidden in unexpected foodstuffs such as tomato sauce, mayonnaise, and sauerkraut, and it's a big part of the rituals surrounding meals and social exchanges (e.g., serving a luscious dessert, bringing candy to a hostess). More to the point, we love it. Sugar is a truly addictive substance, no easier to quit than nicotine. Even cutting down on it is tough. So to bolster your resolve, consider whether the pleasure of that muffin in the morning is really worth suffering pain for. Or that bowl of granola (even "health food" cereals are full of sweetener)? Or that piece of cheesecake or glass of juice? Measure your enjoyment of these treats against your desire to get rid of your pain, and see which weighs heavier in the scale.

Sugar undermines the pain-relieving power of the Ming Method by attaching to the proteins in fascia, triggering a chemical reaction that makes these proteins stiff and tough—the opposite of what you're trying to achieve with the stretches. If this stiffening process goes on for a long time, the body views the affected tissue as foreign and attacks it, leading to an inflammatory reaction.

Sugar Substitutes

If like most of us you can't live without something sweet, look for one of these ingredients on the label.

> **Stevia** comes from the leaves of a naturally sweet plant and is available as a powder or liquid. It's actually far sweeter than sugar; use just a tiny bit to avoid an unpleasant aftertaste.
> **Inositol** is a naturally sweet nutrient found in many plant foods. You can get it as a powder to sprinkle on foods.

Try stevia or inositol first. If you're really unsatisfied and crave a sweeter taste, try one of the following products. However, these products should be used with caution and in very small amounts. Stevia and inositol chemically are not true sugars, but agave and honey are and can make you fat. Your guiding principle should be "minimum amount for maximum pleasure."

> **Agave nectar** is a sweet syrup produced from a type of cactus. Agave doesn't trigger the body to produce insulin, but it can cause weight gain.
> **Raw honey** contains enzymes, trace minerals, and other nutrients. Do not use honey that has been processed by heating. You need only very small amounts—it's sweeter than sugar.

Harden your resolve, go through your cupboards, and toss out everything that looks like cookies, doughnuts, cakes, soda, and juice (even health food juices). All these products have sky-high sugar content. If you must have fruit, eat whole fruit, which includes fiber, the way nature intended you to eat it. But avoid bananas and grapes, which have the highest sugar content of all fruit. (Never eat fruit that's frozen or packed in cans, which usually has sugar *added* to it.)

Yes, it's hard to live without dessert. But you don't have to. I do my dessert shopping in the health food store, finding products that use healthier sugar substitutes. See the sidebar for a list of acceptable sweeteners. Instead of a muffin or Danish in the morning, try a small bowl of organic oatmeal with a few drops of stevia and about a dozen chopped organic almonds or walnuts. Not only will you spare your body some inflammation-promoting sugar, you'll get real nutrition that will keep you going until lunch, without needing a sugary snack at 11 A.M.

Eliminate Trans-Fatty Acids

Starting in 2007, New York City banned the use of trans-fatty acids (TFAs) or trans fats in all its restaurants. TFAs, said the department of health, are an "invisible and dangerous" hazard in food—in fact, the "most dangerous fat." The focus of New York's ban was preventing heart disease. But TFAs cause many other types of damage in the body, and one way they do that is by triggering inflammation, the very thing you want to avoid.

TFAs are created artificially through a chemical process that pumps hydrogen into vegetable oil, producing "partially hydrogenated" oil. Any food fried in partially hydrogenated vegetable oil contains trans fats. So do margarine and vegetable shortening; chips, taco shells, and doughnuts; all sorts of baked goods, including hamburger buns, pizza dough, crackers, cookies, and pies; and ready-to-make mixes, such as for pancakes, biscuits, and hot chocolate.

Frying foods at high temperatures also creates TFAs. Deep-frying is done at high temperatures, so avoid deep-fried foods, including steaks, chicken, French fries, and fish. (Doughnuts pack a double whammy: they're deep-fried *plus* loaded with sugar.) A good rule of thumb in cooking is if the oil smokes, it's too hot.

Given that TFAs are universally condemned by health experts as perhaps the number one most dangerous food, your ideal goal would be to eliminate them from your diet. This would be true even if you didn't have pain, but if you do, you have all the more reason to avoid TFAs like the plague.

In the real world, you have to do the best you can. Even if you can't resist every bag of chips you encounter, reducing the overall number of chips you eat can only benefit your fascia. I frequently go off my diet. But I just forgive myself and then go back on it the next day. The biggest factor preventing people from staying on my program is that after they mess up, they're too hard on themselves. They feel they've totally failed, so they just continue to eat the bad food they were eating when they fell off the wagon. It's much better to simply accept that because you're human, you'll cheat occasionally. A forgiving attitude helps you keep cheating to a minimum.

On special occasions especially, allow yourself to eat more liberally, but keep a little pilot light burning in the back of your mind. When I go on vacation or to a party, barbecue, or family gathering, I anticipate that I'm going to eat anything that's there. I do feel bad about it—but I enjoy every bite. Then I go home and eat perfectly to clean out my system.

Add Anti-Inflammatory Foods to Your Diet

The three foods that follow have anti-inflammatory properties. Eating them actually helps heal your fascia.

> **Tart cherries** (also called sour cherries and used for pies and other desserts), unlike sweet cherries, contain substances called anthocyanins, which have an anti-inflammatory effect similar to that of fish oil. If you want to eat fruit, this is a good choice. Buy these cherries dried or fresh in a good health food store or at a farmer's market.
> **Extra-virgin olive oil** contains the anti-inflammatory compound oleocanthal, making this oil an excellent choice for salad dressings and cooking. Be sure to use only cold-pressed, extra-virgin oil.
> **Avocados** contain proteoglycans called aggrecans, which are building blocks of connective tissue, so eating them may help repair inflamed tissue.

Supplementation

Another way to help stack the odds in your favor is by using anti-inflammatory supplements, plus supplements that provide additional support for your joints. Don't skip these supplements—they're integral to the program.

Fish Oil

My favorite supplement for reducing inflammation is fish oil. The oils from mackerel, tuna, sardines, and cod are rich in omega-3 fatty acids, a type of fat essential to the body, but which our normal diet is deficient in. (A new, especially rich source of omega-3s is krill, an arctic shrimplike creature.)

Fish Oil Burns Fat

An added benefit of fish oil is that if you use it longer than six weeks, it helps you burn fat. My patient Karen resisted the instruction to take omega-3s because she thought that two tablespoons of fish oil a day was too many calories and she'd get fat—a fearsome thing to her. So I explained the well-known chemical concept that the burning of fat is enhanced by the presence of fish oil, and she reluctantly agreed to try the fish oil. As it turned out, Karen didn't gain any weight—in fact, she lost a bit.

Much research indicates that omega-3 fatty acid supplements block production of chemicals called prostaglandins that create pain and inflammation. Based on studies of teeth, scientists have learned that Paleolithic humans consumed 3,000 milligrams of omega-3s a day. Americans, by contrast, take in only 120 milligrams a day, on average. We are far behind on the amount of omega-3s we should be consuming, and it's a major problem.

The best way to get fish oil is by supplementation. Because of pollution with heavy metals such as mercury, arsenic, and cadmium, and other poisons such as PCBs (polychlorinated biphenyls) and dioxin, it's hard to get your omega-3s safely from the actual fish anymore. The cleanest, best fish to eat is wild Alaskan salmon. Two 4-ounce servings of it per week give you the minimum amount of omega-3s needed by someone who has no health problems. But if you have any type of pain or inflammatory condition, you need omega-3s every day, and most people don't want to eat fish every day.

Fish oil is available as gelcaps or liquid. Buy it from a company that certifies it to be free of rancidity and contaminants such as mercury and PCBs. Call the company and ask to see their documentation on this. What you want is "pharmaceutical grade" fish oil, meaning that the product is very pure, free of contaminants, and in the best case, tested by an independent lab. Drug companies have come up with their own pharmaceutical-grade fish oils that require a doctor's prescription and are quite costly. You will do just as well to buy high-quality oil from a health food store or online. Three companies I trust are Nordic Naturals,

Fish Oil Cautions

> One effect of fish oil is to thin the blood, so if you have a bleeding disorder or are taking a blood-thinning medication such as Coumadin, warfarin, or aspirin therapy, do not take fish oil without consulting a complementary-integrative medical doctor.

> If you think high doses of fish oil might benefit you, consult a complementary-integrative medical doctor who uses substances other than drugs to treat patients. Most conventional doctors have not been trained to use supplements or food as medicine and cannot advise you.

Carlson's, and Life Extension Foundation, which purify the oils by a process called molecular distillation.

Dosages. A good dosage of fish oil to support anyone's general health is 1.5 grams (1,500 mg) per day. Check the label to see how many gelcaps or teaspoons give you that amount. To get an anti-inflammatory effect, however, you need at least 2.5 grams (2,500 mg) per day. People who weigh more than 200 pounds and serious athletes can take even higher doses, but only under the supervision of an alternative practitioner such as a naturopath or a complementary-integrative medical doctor. Some doctors recommend up to 9 grams (9,000 mg) per day in cases of severe fibromyalgia or for professional athletes who weigh more than 200 pounds and are training intensively, although never for more than a few days at a time. I take 3 to 9 grams (3,000 to 9,000 mg), but I don't recommend this amount to other people without knowing the details of their medical condition.

How to Take Fish Oil. Divide the amount of fish oil you're taking into at least two doses a day; three times a day is better, if you can manage it. Take fish oil after a meal, since having food in your stomach lessens the chance that you will experience gas or that the oil will repeat on you. If you do have gas, drop back to a lower dose, such as 500 milligrams twice a day, and slowly build up to a higher dose. Also try taking a digestive enzyme along with the fish oil. These two measures should eliminate any gas problems.

Pain Relief for Athletes

If more athletes only knew it, enzymes give great pain relief. A study published in 2004 in the *Journal of Sports Sciences* found that downhill runners who took a mixture of several systemic enzymes before and after intense exercise had much less muscle soreness than a similar group who did the same exercise but took no enzymes.

Systemic Enzymes

I recommend systemic enzymes as a second anti-inflammatory supplement. These are different from digestive enzymes, which work in the stomach and intestines to aid digestion. Systemic enzymes are so named because they pass through the stomach and intestines and circulate in the blood throughout your system to "digest" scar tissue that has formed in your fascia.

Enzymes are chemicals naturally produced by the body and are responsible for many of its functions. Between ages twenty-seven and thirty-five, the body's enzyme-producing capacity drops dramatically. That's why athletes start losing their skills around that time. Most people older than thirty-five can't produce all the enzymes the body requires. Illness, injury, or poor diet only makes this problem worse. You take systemic enzymes to restore your enzyme levels.

For our purposes, the enzymes' primary role is to circulate through the body and soften or dissolve scar tissue. But they also act like fish oil, by reducing inflammation. In fact, these two supplements work together to decrease pain and increase mobility. Adding enzymes to fish oil is a perfect way to start my program.

Systemic enzymes have other benefits as well. They boost your immune system and deactivate viruses so they can't make you sick. The enzymes also lower blood pressure by dissolving strands of tough tissue that clog up your blood vessels. They're like a Roto-Rooter, cleaning everything out.

A variety of systemic enzyme products are available. (Remember, you want *systemic* enzymes, *not* digestive enzymes.) Look for these ingredients on the label: papain, bromelain, chymotrypsin, amylase, and serrapeptase (also called serratia peptidase and particularly important for eating up scar tissue). Products I like include Wobenzyme by Naturally Vitamins, Intenzyme Forte by Biotics, and Vitalzym by World Nutrition. More potent than Vitalzym is a product called Vitalzym X, but you can get it only through a medical professional. Some of these products may not be in stores, but they are easy to find online. You can also ask the staff in health food stores about other enzyme products; then check the labels to see if they contain at least the first four ingredients listed earlier. (Products containing serrapeptase are harder to find in stores, but you can get serrapeptase by itself and combine it with a product that includes the other enzymes.) Enzymes can be pricey, but I believe they are essential and worth the cost.

Dosages. You need a high dosage of enzymes for the anti-inflammatory effects to kick in. The exact amount depends on which product you take, since strengths vary among manufacturers, but a good general rule is to begin with a low dose (two pills three times a day). Increase the dose gradually, while carefully monitoring how you feel—particularly any changes in the level of your aches and pains. You'll reach a point at which you feel better, called the activation dosage. Continue taking that amount until your pain is manageable, even if it means taking a lot of pills. However, do not take this high dose for longer than a week. Some of my patients have taken as many as ten pills three times a day for severe pain. If you feel you need more than twenty-one pills a day, first consult a naturopath or complementary-integrative medical doctor.

Summary of Enzyme Dosages

> Start with two pills, three times a day.
> Build up to a maximum dosage of twenty-one pills: seven pills three times a day. Do not take this dosage for longer than one week.

> When your pain level has decreased by 20 percent, decrease your dose to three pills, three times a day.
> When your pain is at level 2, decrease the dosage to three pills twice a day, for maintenance.

Enzyme Cautions

> Systemic enzymes thin the blood. So if you are taking blood thinners, *do not* take them without consulting an integrative-complementary medical doctor.

> If you are scheduled for surgery, stop taking enzymes two weeks before the procedure.

> If you have severe kidney or liver disease, *do not* take enzymes without consulting a complementary-integrative medical doctor.

> Systemic enzymes give people a bit of a sour stomach sometimes, but most find these enzymes relatively easy to tolerate. At higher dosages you may experience a detox or cleansing reaction that can involve headaches, aches and pains, nausea, or a general all-over lousy feeling.

This is good! It means the enzymes are clearing out toxins and dead bacteria. But to reduce your discomfort, lower your dose and build up again more gradually. Drinking additional water also can help the cleansing process.

> There is no scientific research investigating whether taking high doses of fish oil and enzymes together over an extended period of time can result in excessive blood thinning. If you think you need to take high doses of both fish oil and enzymes for more than seven days, consult a naturopath or complementary-integrative medical doctor to monitor your blood clotting.

Once your pain level has dropped by 20 percent, decrease the dose to three pills, three times a day. When your pain has dropped to level 2, decrease the dose again to three pills twice a day for maintenance. Those older than thirty-five should stay at this maintenance level for the rest of their life. (If your pain doesn't decrease by 20 percent in response to a high dose of enzymes, consult a naturopath or complementary-integrative medical doctor, since some underlying condition may be causing it.) Unless you are taking blood-thinning medications (see "Enzyme Cautions" sidebar), these enzymes are safe.

How to Take Enzymes. You *must* take systemic enzymes on an empty stomach and by themselves, without any other supplements. If you don't, they will simply digest your food and never make it out into the bloodstream to do the work you want them to do. Ideally, take these enzymes three times a day: one hour before a meal or two hours after a meal. That way you can be sure no food will get in their way.

Many of my patients complain that it's hard to find the strategic moment for taking enzymes in the middle of a workday. I tell them to take their enzymes first thing in the morning, at night just before bed, and one time during the day when their stomach is relatively empty. Although you may not find the perfect moment, it's better to get those enzymes into you, even with some food in your stomach. So don't knock yourself out over it—you'll still benefit.

Joint Health Supplements

To boost your odds to the utmost, I urge you to add to your regimen supplements that specifically support joint tissue. The sidebar on the next page lists nine supplements that work together to repair and protect the cartilage and connective tissue in your joints. They're listed in order of importance, so if you feel overwhelmed at the thought of taking all of them, simply include as many as you can, starting from the top of the list. But remember that you won't benefit as much from a few as you will from all of them working synergistically.

Ideally, look for a single product that contains many or all of these ingredients. It will be more convenient to take, and you'll get the best results. My own favorite product, which I use myself, is Dr. Mauro Di Pasquale's Joint Support, which includes all the ingredients in the sidebar and many more (available online at mdplusstore.com). If you're shopping in a store, ask the salesperson which companies make pharmaceutical-grade products. Some companies I like: NOW Foods, Enzymatic Therapy, Life Extension Foundation, Biotics, and Carlson's.

Finally, if you'd like to add a great cornerstone multinutrient product that makes all the others work better, I recommend Life Extension Mix, which contains more than ninety ingredients (available at lef.org). It removes all the guesswork from taking multivitamins. However, this product won't fix your joints. If you're older than forty, you still need to take joint supplements periodically.

Ming's Recommended Joint Supplements

The first three ingredients in the following list are the big ones: take these products even if you don't take anything else. They go directly into the joints, and combined with fish oil and enzymes, they have a powerful effect.

⟩ **Glucosamine sulfate.** A main constituent of joint tissue that helps rebuild joints by repairing cartilage. Start at a dose of 500 milligrams per day and work up to 1,500 milligrams per day.

⟩ **Chondroitin sulfate.** A major component of cartilage that has a particular ability to attract water into the joint. Your dose of chondroitin should be half your dose of glucosamine.

⟩ **Hyaluronic acid.** An important component of connective tissue that brings water into the joint and provides lubrication and shock absorption. The standard dose for anyone is 100 milligrams per day.

⟩ **Magnesium.** A natural muscle relaxant. Muscles can't be in a relaxed state unless magnesium is present, yet most Americans are deficient in this mineral. I recommend using a product that blends different types of magnesium (e.g., citrate, sulfate, oxide, glycinate, malate) to maximize your body's ability to absorb it. The minimum dose is 500 milligrams.

⟩ **MSM (methylsulfonylmethane).** A natural form of sulfur that the body needs to make connective tissue. It can reduce scar tissue and inflammation. My recommended dose is 1,000 milligrams per day.

⟩ **Vitamin C.** Well-known as an antioxidant that prevents cell damage, vitamin C helps prevent joint inflammation. It must be present for tissue to heal. The minimum dose is 1,000 milligrams per day.

⟩ **NAC (N-acetyl cysteine).** An amino acid (building block of protein) that works together with vitamin C to reduce inflammation and tissue damage. The minimum dose is 600 milligrams per day.

⟩ **Carnosine.** An amino acid that helps prevent the stiffening of connective tissue and protects against age-related degeneration of protein, including fascia. You must use it for at least two months to create a protective effect. The minimum dose is 500 milligrams twice a day.

⟩ **Boswellia extract.** An herbal product that prevents the breakdown of connective tissue by reducing inflammation. My recommended dose is 300 milligrams per day.

Into the Future

Even after you fix your pain problem, you still need fish oil and enzymes. I recommend that you keep taking them in low dosages for the rest of your life. And never slack up on your water drinking. When I don't drink enough water, my shoulder gets a bit stiff.

As for the joint supplements, anyone forty or younger can get away with using them only as needed—that is, when you have a joint or pain problem. People older than forty should take these supplements periodically, even if they have no problems. I recommend taking them for a month, three times a year, at the standard, minimal dosages listed in the sidebar. Feeling creaky is a signal that it's time to do this.

Don't Drive Before You Tune Up

Think of your body as a car that hasn't had a tune-up for the last ten years. Would you ever drive a car like that? I wouldn't. My preparatory program actually makes you your own mechanic, repairing little dings as well as major problems in the engine. Once you get your car to the point where it's drivable, you can start driving very slowly: beginning the stretching program. Then you can drive at normal speeds: strength training to gain muscle mass. That way, you'll get all systems into shape before you embark on the Indy 500: explosive strength training. By preparing your tissue in this systematic, scientific way, you're giving yourself the best car possible to drive, and you reduce your odds that accidents (e.g., twisting your ankle when you run or lifting a heavy object and pulling a muscle) will happen down the road.

CHAPTER FIVE

Testing Your Readiness

Learning to Communicate with Your Body

A s you complete the preparatory program, you'll use the simple indications in this chapter to determine for yourself when your tissue is ready to stretch. The very first thing to do, however, *before beginning your preparatory program*, is to establish a benchmark by creating a description of your pain.

Rating Your Pain Level

I never touch new patients without first asking them to rate their pain level on a scale of 0 to 10. This is essential for working with your pain, and I urge you to do it.

Before drinking a single cup of water, write a paragraph describing how your pain feels and how it looks. By "looks," I mean how it affects your posture. For example, if you have lower-back pain, your body may be twisted. Observe yourself in the mirror and note, "OK, my hip is rotated to the right, and it's also tilted to the right." Jot that down. Then give your pain a number on a scale from 0 to 10 (use the guidelines in the sidebar). Last, write a description of it. Is the pain more intense in the morning? At night? Does your back hurt when you get up after sitting for an hour or more? Use ranges of numbers if you like. For example, you can say that your pain ranges from level 2 in the morning to level 4 at night. You might also want to have someone take front, side, and back pictures of you. Hang on to the photos, and compare them to what you look like a few weeks later. You'll see a change.

Now begin the preparatory program. At the end of the ten days, pull out the paragraph you wrote and use it to help decide whether you're ready to stretch. After two to three weeks of stretching, take the paragraph out again and see how what you wrote then compares with how you feel now. Does your back still hurt after sitting for an hour? Do you have the same level of pain when you get up in the morning? Repeat this comparison after another three weeks.

You need a written benchmark because changes resulting from the program are often subtle. Even though a 2 percent improvement each day adds up to a major change over thirty days, many people don't realize how much they've actually improved. Diane, an attractive, in-shape thirty-six-year-old, came to me with broad, diffuse pains running from the front of her hip to her buttock to her lower back and knee on the right side. After a couple of weeks, she reported that her hip pain had decreased only from level 4 to 3.5. But when I questioned her further, it turned out she had neglected to mention that her knee and lower-back pain had disappeared completely. That was an overall improvement of 50 percent: everything

Ming's Pain Scale

Use these guidelines to decide which number from 0 to 10 best describes your pain level.

0 = no pain

1 = a ghost of a pain

2 = pain that's more than a nuisance. You're slightly concerned about it but not overly worried. You can get through the day without painkillers. But it impairs optimum performance in sporting activities.

5 = the threshold of real injury. Your pain impairs your ability to function. If you have lower-back pain, you start to limp; if someone bumps into you, it takes your breath away; and bending forward is painful and laborious. This is the point where your pain starts making you worry.

10 = maximum, excruciating pain. You can do nothing but go home, take a painkiller, and apply an ice pack. You don't want to be bothered by anyone or anything.

surrounding the hip pain was dramatically better. Pain actually distorts your perception; to make sure you gauge your improvement accurately, you need both a verbal description of your pain and a number level.

Stop Taking Painkillers!

When a new patient calls me, one of the first questions I ask is, "Are you on pain medications or muscle relaxants?" If someone is taking these drugs, my initial evaluation will be inaccurate. Therefore, I tell the patient to consult with his or her doctor to find a safe way to get off the medication for three days so I can evaluate the patient properly.

If you want to pinpoint the nature of your own pain, you can't be taking painkillers. They mask your symptoms, which means you'll never discover your true pain level. So if you've been taking prescription painkillers or muscle relaxants—or using ibuprofen, aspirin, or another over-the-counter pain remedy—you must stop taking it for three days before doing your assessment. Be prepared for your pain level to go up. This will not be pleasant, but put up with it for three days—both to get an accurate assessment and to help you realize just how much the drugs have been masking your true pain level.

To my mind, powerful muscle relaxants and anti-inflammatory drugs are the doctors' easy button, which they push to hide everything that's wrong. But over time, the effects can be devastating. The drugs deactivate the pain detectors in an injured joint, but since the fascial restrictions are still present, even normal movement creates damage without your being aware of it. Due to this unperceived tissue damage, the pain level you experience when you stop the drugs may actually be higher than your original pain level. The drugs seem to put out the fire of inflammation, but often after you get off them, you find yourself left with the charred remains of your unhappy tissues. My advice is never play any sport or do any training under the influence of painkillers or muscle relaxants—and that includes the over-the-counter drugs. It's the fastest way to disintegrate a joint. If you use painkillers to keep playing golf, for example, you'll tear your back to shreds.

Unfortunately, drugs are the standard treatment for pain in this country. But in the Ming world, you can try a whole universe of therapies before you start to think about pain medication. As described in Chapter 4, they include fish oil, water, and enzymes. This combination often has the same pain-reducing effect as the drugs—except, of course, it's much safer. If you discover that hydration, fish oil, and enzymes reduce your pain to an acceptable level, consider stopping your pain medications entirely—with your doctor's permission, if you're taking prescription drugs. If your doctor isn't aware of the uses of these supplements, consult a complementary-integrative medical doctor who understands drugs as well as alternative care.

If your pain is so bad that it prevents you from sleeping, you have to keep using your medications just to survive, but you won't get an accurate pain assessment. In such a situation, you simply have to work with what's possible. Once you start the fish oil, hydration, and enzymes, your pain will begin decreasing, and with the guidance of a complementary-integrative medical doctor, you can carefully and seamlessly make the transition, gradually decreasing the medications and increasing the supplements.

Am I Ready to Stretch?

As the tenth day of preparation approaches, you're probably already feeling better. But how do you know you're *really* ready to stretch? Fortunately, there's little guesswork involved. Just look for a few definitive signs.

> **Less pain.** The big sign is that your pain level, as measured by the pain scale, is 20 to 30 percent lower—often including a pain reduction in parts of your body that you never even thought of as "painful." When Theresa came to me with lower-back and hip pain, I put her on the preparatory program. After ten days, she felt generally "looser," as she put it. "My neck used to be tight," she remarked, "and now it's not stiff. I don't know why." Of course, I knew why: water, enzymes, and fish oil don't target just the painful parts, *they benefit the entire body*. As a result, areas that weren't actually painful but felt slightly "off" now feel fine. A vague discomfort that registered as 0.5 on the pain scale improves to 0.

> **A greater sense of general well-being.** You notice overall improvement in your sleep, elimination, and other body functions. How you feel when you wake up in the morning is a good barometer. Once you're fully awake, do you feel energetic, rather than achy or sluggish? Since water is involved in every chemical reaction in the body, it makes sense that your body works better when it's fully hydrated—and when it does, you have more energy.

> **A change in the quality and texture of your skin, particularly in your face.** The benefits of hydration, enzymes, and fish oil combine to make you look younger and healthier. People who haven't seen you in a while remark, "Hey, you look different!" This happens to quite a few of my patients.

> **Improvement in mobility.** Your mobility is better even though you haven't done any stretching yet. Do your own unique test: pick one or two problematic joints and test them before your ten days of preparation; then test them again after. For example, if you have trouble raising your arm above your head, do a test raise before you begin the program and make a note of how high the arm can go. Shoulder level? Up to your ear? Test again after the ten days. Invariably there's an improvement. The preparatory program is almost like a stretch in a bottle.

> **A change in your body overall.** When you take off your clothes, your entire body looks more supple and robust. Your muscles look smoother and fuller; your stomach is flatter. These changes are subtle but definite.

> **A change in your stool.** The stool itself is softer, and you don't need to bear down as forcefully to void. The frequency of stools increases. Ideally the stool should float, indicating a higher water content. This means that you're hydrating successfully.

> **Your urine is clear and relatively odorless.** Light, clear urine indicates more water in the body. (Note: B vitamins turn urine yellow, so you need to briefly stop taking them to see if your urine has become lighter.)

> **Your mental function and mood improve.** When you're dehydrated and lacking omega-3s, you don't think clearly. When you're constipated, you're more likely to be grumpy. When these conditions reverse, you naturally feel more upbeat.

Your body will talk to you through these little improvements. However, changes appear gradually, and because you look at yourself every day, you might not see improvements clearly (although other people will notice a difference). So before beginning the preparatory program, make notes on each of the preceding points, in addition to writing your pain paragraph. Then revisit your notes after ten days on the preparatory program, and see what's changed.

Some people need more than ten days of preparation. Often this is because they aren't drinking enough water or taking large enough doses of enzymes and fish oil. Other people have conditions involving more severe inflammation and must continue the preparatory program for a longer period until the inflammation subsides. (See the sidebar "Stretching with an Inflammatory Condition," on page 79, for details.) A good rule of thumb for everyone is not to stretch if your body feels hypersensitive to any type of movement.

The bottom line is there'll be a moment when you say, "You know, I feel pretty good! I'm ready!" That's the moment to begin stretching.

Whatever your condition, if you're in any doubt about doing my program or your problem is complicated, consult a naturopath or complementary-integrative medical doctor about whether the stretches are OK for you. In my own experience, as long as people follow the preparatory program so that their tissue is adequately hydrated and minimally inflamed, doing the stretches has never injured anyone.

Learning to Read Your Body

Determining for yourself whether you're ready to stretch should help embed in your brain the idea that *you can learn to read your body.* Your body tells you a lot, as in the sign noted previously of feeling more energetic when you wake up in the morning. People tend to rely too much on high-tech diagnostic tests. If I feel lousy, I know I'm not well. I don't need a doctor to tell me this. By the same token, you *know* when you're feeling better—you just need to pay attention.

All the technology we live with has disconnected us from our physical being. We've forgotten that nature's profound intelligence gave us our body—it's not simply another machine to be manipulated by technology—and we've lost the ability to communicate with it. Most people are so disconnected from their bodies that they actually have no clue when their problems are improving—like Diane, who was so focused on her hip pain that she completely forgot that her knee and back pain was totally gone and only remembered when I questioned her. As if she couldn't believe that complete relief was possible, she didn't perceive it when it actually happened. If you're one of these disconnected types—or suspect you may be—rely on a mate, loved one, or close friend, who most likely can detect changes more accurately than you can yourself.

The moral is you must maintain an open mind. If you find yourself feeling better, accept it—don't fight it. For me, the best patient is an optimistic person who wants to get better and remains hopeful. A neutral patient is OK, too. This person says, "I'm skeptical, but I'll listen to your argument and give it a try." The worst patient is the one who just won't believe that getting better is possible—even when the pain decreases. This person has been brainwashed to believe that the only way to fix problems is with drugs and surgery. If you've been entertaining such thoughts, try to put them aside just for these ten days. Write down your before-and-after observations as I suggested earlier. If at the end of ten days you find yourself feeling better, you'll have your own evidence that the conventional medical model doesn't have all the answers.

Who Should *Not* Stretch

In a few situations, stretching is not appropriate. *Do not* do either the spinal release stretches or the fascial stretches if:

> You have an obvious bone fracture.
> You have bone cancer.
> You're pregnant.
> You have a recent muscle, ligament, or tendon tear; an acutely sprained ankle; a whiplash injury; or a contusion injury (e.g., from being hit by a baseball) with obvious bruising and swelling. Wait until the pain and inflammation subside. One of my patients had a partially torn calf muscle. He stretched it, and it tore some more. Be sure to wait at least three weeks before you stretch a partially torn muscle (i.e., one with only a couple of torn fibers) to give it time to heal. For torn tendons or ligaments, or severely torn muscles, you must consult an orthopedic M.D. to find out how severe the tear is. These tears should never be stretched until totally healed, and you need a doctor to tell you when this has occurred.

Stretching with an Inflammatory Condition

If you have a systemic inflammation, as in fibromyalgia, rheumatoid arthritis, and other inflammatory diseases, you can stretch even if you are on prednisone or other anti-inflammatory drugs. But for you the preparatory program is especially critical to minimize the inflammation before you begin. Use this simple test to determine whether your tissue is ready to stretch.

1. Find a joint that's sore.
2. Touch it, and write down a number from 0 to 10 that describes the pain level.
3. Follow my preparatory program for ten to fourteen days.

4. Test the pain level again. If the joint is 30 to 50 percent improved, you can stretch. If your condition is severe, you may need longer than ten to fourteen days to get this much improvement.

You may find that your condition rapidly improves with the Ming Method. If it does, and you are taking anti-inflammatory drugs, consult your doctor about whether it would be appropriate for you to reduce your dosages to decrease the chances of long-term side effects.

The single most important lesson this book can teach you is how to communicate with your body. Learning to read the signals it sends is the first step in treating your pain successfully; it is part of the empowerment offered by the Ming Method. Once you can observe the pain precisely, you can approach it without being clouded by emotional reactions. You'll have a clearer, more objective picture of what measures you need to treat your pain, plus a technique for evaluating whether an approach is working.

In his book *How Doctors Think*, Jerome Groopman, M.D., notes that most doctors do not listen to a patient describing symptoms for longer than eighteen seconds. He connects this with the fact that as many as 15 percent of diagnoses are incorrect. Patients feel ignored, and treatment results can be disastrous. In the Ming Method, by contrast, you actively participate in your own healing—and you will certainly devote more than eighteen seconds to your own assessment.

CHAPTER SIX

The Spinal Stretches

The spinal stretches you're about to learn definitely are bizarre. They look weird and feel weird, too, until that moment of clarity: "Oh! That's what he's talking about!" Keep in mind that these peculiar positions are designed to stretch long sheets of fascial tissue extending through large areas of your body, to create a type of release you have never achieved before. In the beginning, you'll probably experience some frustration, but stay with it. If you make it past just the first week or so, there's a tipping point at which your body suddenly understands what it's doing.

Stretching tight, constricted fascia is uncomfortable at the beginning. So start out with a firm, focused intention and a willingness to face discomfort and put in a strong effort. This program is not easy. You are doing it because the rewards are tremendous. Your goal is to reach a point where these stretches are a part of you, a deeply ingrained routine like brushing your teeth.

Over time as your fascia starts to release and elongate, stretching becomes much easier. You'll find that the strength to hold the stretches for a full sixty seconds develops quite rapidly. My patients often feel frustrated at first because they can't maintain a stretch very long. They assume this is because their muscles are weak, and that's partly true. But equally important, their spinal nerves aren't sending full-strength signals to those muscles. Within a few days, as the stretching creates some space between the vertebrae, they suddenly discover a new strength that comes purely from fully functioning nerves.

General Instructions for Spinal Stretching

Begin the spinal and fascial stretches on the same day. You don't have to do both kinds at the same time, although you can if that's convenient for you. But you should do *all* the stretches in your program *every* day. Here are several basic guidelines:

> Stretch on a relatively soft surface, such as a carpet with a fair amount of cushioning or an exercise mat that's about ½-inch thick—not on a hard surface such as a wood floor. Take your shoes off.

> Your body should be moderately warm before you stretch. "Moderately warm" means that if you feel cold or even chilly, you're not warm enough. Your body should feel loose. Don't stretch right after you've come in from the cold! Do the stretches in a warm room, with a sweatshirt on. When you have the opportunity, it's especially effective to stretch after using a sauna or hot tub, or even after taking a hot bath or shower. Drink a cup of water right after the shower or sauna, wait a few minutes so the water can pass through your digestive tract, and then stretch. Other good moments are after a massage, when your fascia is already softened up, and when you're warm after a workout.

> The ideal time of day to do the spinal stretches—especially if you have chronic or severe pain—is right before you climb into bed at night, because being horizontal helps maintain the spaces the stretches create between vertebrae. As soon as your body is upright, the spine starts to compress, but when you're lying down, it stays open. Let's say I have lower-back compression that's causing an ankle problem. I do the Low Back Stretch and go straight to bed. Because I'm horizontal all night, the nerves in my lower back remain uncompressed, sending stronger signals to the leg and foot, buying time for healing to occur in the joint. By the end of the next day, my lower back will be compressed again, but if I stretch regularly every night, little by little my ankle will heal.

> Always do spinal stretches that affect the higher parts of the body before those that affect the lower parts. Thus neck stretches come before mid-back stretches, which come before lower-back stretches.

> If you can, stretch in front of a mirror. Since you won't have Ming Chew correcting your position, you need something to give you feedback. You can also try a mental device I use. I keep an endless tape loop running in my mind: Are my legs straight? Are my feet flexed? The instructions for each stretch include a "Tape Loop," which gives you the cues to scan for as you do the stretch. Keep the tape loop going in your mind for the entire sixty seconds. At the beginning, you'll need to keep this book nearby so you can keep checking which items to bear in mind. After about six sessions, however, you'll find that your body "gets" the stretches, and you'll be able to remember the contents of the tape loop.

Timing the Stretches

Hold all the spinal stretches for a full sixty seconds. This is done for two reasons: First, you need to hold the fascia in tension for a certain length of time to reshape it. Second, the spinal stretches actually create suction that draws water into the fascia and the spinal disk, and this takes the full sixty seconds to occur. If you can't hold for an entire minute at the beginning, start at forty-five seconds, thirty, or even fifteen, and work up to sixty gradually.

The sixty-second total *includes* the time it takes you to settle into position, so start counting as soon as you begin getting into the stretch. Beginners need twenty to thirty seconds to do this, but don't worry—it's been factored in. As you gain experience, you lock into position within five to ten seconds, so the amount of actual therapeutic time increases.

There are a number of ways to keep time. I stretch next to a clock with a second hand and check it periodically. You can use a timer, or count inside your head. One patient told me that she counts her breaths.

"Flashing In and Out"

You'll find that some spinal stretches are easy, and you can hold them for sixty seconds after only two or three sessions. Other stretches are difficult and take longer to master. The general principle is that the spinal stretches you find the hardest are the ones you need to work on the most. In fact, this is how you diagnose your own problem. Since each stretch releases a particular region of the spine that's related to a specific part of the body, the difficulty of each stretch tells you whether there's a problem in the general area it relates to. Then you can use the fascial stretches to find out which specific muscles in that part of the body are affected.

Most people can't hold the spinal stretches for sixty seconds when they first try them—in fact, thirty seconds is a long time to hold at the beginning. I've discovered that dancers, women, and thin people in general can do the stretches more easily than older people, overweight people, those with a lot of injuries, and men. Men are generally less flexible than women and usually have a body type—especially a stocky or muscular build—that makes it harder to hold a stretch. When I started out, I couldn't do the Low Back Stretch for more than twenty seconds, and it's still challenging for me. For people who are not very flexible or have difficulty getting down on the floor, I've included easier versions of most of the stretches, which can be done on a chair or cushion until you develop the ability to do the regular versions.

Another important point: even once a stretch has become easy for you, *do not expect yourself to hold it perfectly for the full sixty seconds*. Your goal is to maintain each piece of the position throughout that minute, but the truth

Visualizing as You Stretch

When you see something clearly in your mind, it starts to happen. Visualization is a well-known technique used in many areas of life, and it works well in the Ming Method. Make it the last part of the tape loop. When I do the spinal stretches, I go through the reminders on my tape loop and finish by visualizing the spine as it's pictured in my anatomy textbook. I imagine my vertebrae separating and the spaces between them enlarging. (Then I start again from the beginning of the tape loop.) In the instructions for the stretches, I tell you what part of the spine each stretch affects so you can visualize for yourself the area you're opening up (refer to Figure 3-1 on page 37).

If you like, you can do an even more complete visualization that takes in several changes at once. As explained earlier, a spinal stretch sucks water into the fascia and disk. So in your mind, visualize the spaces opening as the vertebrae separate, water flowing into the area, and pressure being released from the compressed nerves.

is that no one, other than a professional dancer, can really do this. Instead, once you're in position, run your tape loop in your mind, continually scanning your body and adjusting each part in turn, maintaining the position to the maximum of your ability. I call this "flashing in and out." Say your right foot relaxes instead of staying flexed. When it comes up on your tape loop, you notice this and flex that foot again. Expect to lose pieces of the stretch even as you strive to maintain as much of it as you can. Just keep scanning and recorrecting yourself. Time for making these changes is built into the sixty seconds.

You'll find these mental devices very helpful. When you use them, you're really willing your body to get better—and it will respond.

It's Not Enough Unless You Vibrate!

Remember that real exertion is essential to stretching successfully. Especially at the beginning, you must work hard enough to make your

In-Flight Stretching

On a plane to Europe, after sitting for several hours, I felt lousy. My backside was as flat as a pancake, my psoas short and tight, my lower back sore, and I had a slight headache. So I got up, drank 8 ounces of water, and stretched in the back of the plane.

I started with a warm-up: slow jogging for thirty seconds (marching in place is another good one for airplanes), 15 reps of standing leg curls (facing the wall, you bend each leg up), 15 reps of standing calf raises (raising up and down on the toes, which flushes blood out of the calves and feet), 12 full squats, and torso rotations with hands on hips (5 reps in each direction). Total time: two minutes, thirty seconds.

Then I stretched my psoas, all three hamstrings, my quadriceps, and my lats (i.e., the large, flat back muscles that go from the lower back to the armpit on each side)—one minute on each side. Total time: eight minutes. I drank 16 more ounces of water, poured another cup, and stood sipping it in the back of the plane for another half hour.

The passengers nearby thought I was crazy, but it really helped. Halfway through the routine I started feeling better, and when I was done I felt dramatically different. Most of my pain disappeared, and my mood changed from grumpy and headachy to pretty good.

body vibrate at least a little. Some people shake like crazy. That's a good sign—it means that you're maximizing the intensity of your muscle contraction, which is necessary for adequate spinal decompression. As you get stronger and your body comes to understand what it's doing, you won't vibrate as much, which indicates that your body is accepting the posture. This learning process occurs for every stretch. If you slack off for a while, the vibration will return until you're up to speed again.

Another caution: once you've become used to the stretches, it's easy to slip into a halfhearted way of doing them. For example, if you're extending your arm, remember that you're not just casually holding it out there. You're pushing as hard as you possibly can, as though you need to save yourself by keeping a heavy weight from crushing you. This goes for extending the legs, head—everything. You need this powerful exertion to activate Sherrington's law. If you do the stretch only halfheartedly, you won't create the separation between vertebrae that you're aiming for.

Chin-Tucked Head Position

Many of the Ming Method stretches require placing your head in a specific, chin-tucked position that's designed both to decompress the vertebrae in the neck and to tether one of the end points of a fascial chain. (The other end point is the feet, which is why many stretches require you to flex your feet.) The head position is critical to the success of those stretches. There's a learning curve to performing the position correctly, especially when you're lying on your back. The detailed instructions that follow apply to all the spinal stretches in this chapter, as well as to a number of fascial stretches in Chapter 7.

Whether you're in a vertical or a horizontal position, the basic concept is to tuck your chin into your neck, creating a double-chin effect, but *without bending your head forward*. You actually want your head to move *backward* slightly, so it's in a straight line with your spine.

First try it sitting upright. Begin by tucking your chin into the bottom of your neck, as though you're making a double chin. The goal is to move your chin toward the notch at the bottom of your neck. It won't actually reach that notch, because you don't want your head to tilt forward. Instead, move your head slightly backward until the back of your neck flattens out. The challenge is to keep your head in a straight line with your spine while tucking your chin directly into your neck. This is what elongates the back of the neck, which is the goal of the head position (see Figures 6-1 and 6-2).

Once your chin is tucked, imagine the top of your head moving away from your shoulders.

It helps to think of your spine and skull as one unit, with the skull a natural extension of the spine. (Notice how the back of the neck and back of the head in Figure 6.1 form a straight line.) Imagine a hook on top of your head and someone pulling your head toward the ceiling.

People tend to drop their jaw by opening their mouth, instead of tucking their chin in. This is incorrect. Keep your lips together, but don't clench your jaw. Remember that all you're doing is pressing your head back.

Now lie on your back and try the head position again, bringing your chin toward the notch at the bottom of your neck. To do this, your head has to come up off the floor. Focus on keeping your spine in a straight line from

FIGURE 6-1
> Correct

FIGURE 6-2
> Incorrect

the top of your head to your sacrum (the triangular bone at the bottom of your spine), and you will find the distance between your head and the floor that's right for your body.

This time, imagine the top of your head moving away from your shoulders, parallel to the floor, and your sacrum moving in the opposite direction. You want to feel a significant amount of tension from the back of your skull down to your lower neck (see Figure 6-3).

The tendency is to lift the head too far above the floor (see Figure 6-4). To prevent this, periodically lower your head and touch it to the ground to make sure it's at the right height.

Most people need to hold their head 1 to 1½ inches above the floor, but the right distance actually is slightly different for everyone. If you are muscular or overweight, your head might be 3 inches off the floor; if you're thin and small, it could be just ½ inch. Find the distance that enables you to maintain that straight line along the spine and back of the head. Ask someone to observe you to make sure your head doesn't bend forward or backward but remains in a completely straight, neutral position. You can ask this person to measure the distance from the back of your head to the floor, to give you a sense of where your head needs to be.

As you hold the head position, maintain a poker face. This is tough! The natural tendency when exerting a lot of effort is to screw up your face. But don't tense your facial muscles. Believe it or not, tightening the face takes you away from your concentration on the stretch. Instead, you want to focus your attention internally. This actually makes the stretch more effective.

If the muscles in the front of your neck aren't strong, you'll find it quite difficult to hold the head position while lying on your back. Don't be discouraged. It's remarkable how quickly those muscles will spring into shape, so persevere. If you can hold for just fifteen seconds at the beginning, so be it. Very soon you'll be up to the full minute.

FIGURE 6-3
❯ Correct

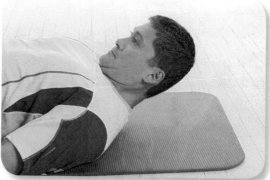

FIGURE 6-4
❯ Incorrect

Some people feel pressure in their head while holding. This is normal. Make sure you don't hold your breath, but keep your breathing going smoothly.

There's a tendency to get distracted by other parts of a stretch and lose the head position, so your tape loop should include a reminder to notice where your head is. Close your eyes and communicate with your neck, imagining that you can feel the neck elongating and the spaces opening up between the vertebrae.

TAPE LOOP

❯ Is my jaw relaxed?
❯ Are my whole head and face relaxed?
❯ Is my neck elongated?
❯ Is my head in the right place? (Lower your head to touch the floor and see where it is.)
❯ Imagine there's a hook on top of your head, and someone's pulling it toward the ceiling.
❯ Imagine the top of your head moving away from your shoulders, parallel to the floor, and your sacrum moving in the opposite direction.
❯ Imagine that you can feel your neck elongating and the spaces opening up between the vertebrae.

WHAT IT SHOULD FEEL LIKE

When the head is in just the right position—whether you're upright or lying down—you can feel the back of the head as an extension of the spine. It's an unmistakable feeling that the spine and head are one elongated column, and when you feel it, you'll know your head is where it belongs.

Dead Roach 1

Named for what you look like while you're doing it, this stretch affects the middle of the neck (i.e., the space between the vertebrae known as C4 and C5; C is for *cervical*, meaning the neck section of the spine). This stretch is for shoulder and rotator cuff problems.

Lie on your back with your knees bent and your feet flat on the floor. First, establish the head position: tuck your chin into the front of your neck, flatten out the back of your neck, and imagine the top of your head moving away from your shoulders.

Now stretch one arm toward the ceiling with the elbow straight (or as straight as you can make it). Bend your wrist so your palm faces the ceiling; then rotate the arm outward so the fingers point toward your *feet* (or as close to that direction as possible). Push the heel of the hand strongly toward the ceiling, with the intention of pulling the arm away from the shoulder joint and creating space in the joint. Then do the same with the other arm. Last, pull your shoulders down toward your hips.

FIGURE 6-5
> Everting foot

Even if you can't actually pull the arm away from the joint, the intent has to be there.

Raise one leg, bringing the knee up as high as you need to in order to flatten out your lower back. (This knee position differs for different people.) Bend your knee at a 90-degree angle and flex the foot so the toes bend toward your face. Last, keeping the toes flexed, tilt the foot so its *outer* edge is closer to you than the *inner* edge. This is called everting the foot; see Figure 6-5.

These movements are subtle and a bit complicated. It may take a few sessions to get them all correct. The important thing is to maintain a clear intention and visual picture of what each part of the leg and foot should be doing. Then after a while your body will follow through.

FIGURE 6-6

Hold that leg in place, and repeat the same movement with the other leg. Keep both heels and knees about 6 inches apart (see Figure 6-6).

You may have difficulty keeping your legs parallel. This is probably because your hips are tight. You can use the Human Pinwheel stretch and Hamstring Spectrum to release this tightness.

EASY VERSION: *If you can't keep your feet in the air, leave your heels on the floor but bend and tilt your feet as described earlier. This position is not as effective as the regular one, because it doesn't flatten out the lower spine properly, but it's a good starting point. As soon as you can, switch to the full stretch with feet raised.*

Now with everything in position, imagine that the bottom of your buttocks and the top of your head are moving in opposite directions. Work to push your buttocks away from your head. *At the same time,* push the heels of your palms toward the ceiling, creating space in the shoulder joint, while *not* raising your head but continuing to move it away from your shoulders. Hold for the remainder of the sixty seconds, or as long as you can.

Moving your buttocks away from your head isn't easy, but keep it as your intention.

At first you won't be able to elongate the spine and also push your palms toward the ceiling without raising your head. But keep imagining these movements happening, and pretty soon they will.

To release the stretch, put your hands behind your head, cradle it gently, and softly let it down onto the floor. **Important:** *do not* just let your head drop. Use your hands to lower it gently.

TAPE LOOP

> Is my head too high? Is my chin tucked strongly into my neck? (Keep dropping your head to different levels to get a sense of where it is in relation to the floor.)
> Are my knees at the right height to keep my lower back flat on the floor?
> Are my feet tilted correctly?
> Are my fingertips pointing toward my feet?
> Am I strongly pushing my hands toward the ceiling while not raising my head?
> Am I pulling my shoulders toward my hips?
> Imagine that your neck is made of supple taffy, which is slowly being pulled and elongated.

WHAT IT SHOULD FEEL LIKE

When you first get into position for Dead Roach 1, your body takes a few seconds to settle into place. Then you get an "aha" moment when the stretch locks in and you feel its specific effects. During the second thirty seconds, usually you feel a dramatic stretch in the middle part of your neck. But remember that you won't get this effect for several sessions—so please stay with it. In the beginning, this stretch may feel rather uncomfortable, but by your sixth session it will seem more normal.

Dead Roach 2

This stretch is the same as Dead Roach 1, except that the different arm position decompresses the space between the vertebrae known as C6 and C7, in the lower part of the neck (C is for *cervical*, meaning the neck section of the spine). Dead Roach 2 strengthens weak triceps or biceps. It also benefits the elbows, wrists, and fingers.

Lie on your back with your knees bent and your feet flat on the floor. Establish the head position: tuck your chin into the front of your neck, flatten out the back of your neck, and imagine the top of your head moving away from your shoulders.

Now stretch your arms down alongside your body. Turn the inside creases of your elbows outward as far as you can. Bend your wrists backward, so your palms face your feet. Your fingers point out to the side. Hold your arms at a 45-degree angle from your body, slightly above the floor so your fingertips barely skim the floor. Push the heels of your palms away from your shoulders as hard as you can. At the same time, pull your shoulders down toward your hips.

Raise one leg, bringing the knee up as high as you need to in order to flatten out your lower back. (This knee position differs for different people.) Bend your knee at a 90-degree angle and flex the foot so the toes bend toward your face. Last, keeping the toes flexed, tilt the foot so its *outer* edge is closer to you than the *inner* edge. This is called everting the foot; see Figure 6-5 on page 90.

It may take a few sessions to get these subtle, slightly complicated movements all correct. Maintain a clear intention and visual picture of what each part of the leg and foot should be doing, and after a while, your body will follow through.

Hold that leg in place, and repeat the same movements with the other leg. Keep both heels and knees about 6 inches apart (see Figure 6-7).

You may have difficulty keeping your legs parallel. This is probably because your hips are tight. You can use the Human Pinwheel stretch and Hamstring Spectrum to release this tightness.

FIGURE 6-7

EASY VERSION: *If you can't keep your feet in the air, leave your heels on the floor but bend and tilt your feet as described earlier. This position is not as effective as the regular one, because it doesn't flatten out the lower spine properly, but it's a good starting point. As soon as you can, switch to the full stretch with feet raised.*

With everything in position, imagine that the bottom of your buttocks and the top of your head are moving in opposite directions. *At the same time*, push the heels of your palms toward your feet and pull your shoulders toward your hips. Hold everything for the rest of the sixty seconds, or as long as you can.

Moving your buttocks away from your head isn't easy, but keep this as your intention.

To release the stretch, put your hands behind your head, cradle it gently, and softly let it down onto the floor. **Important:** *do not* just let your head drop. Use your hands to lower it gently.

TAPE LOOP

> Is my chin tucked strongly into my neck? Is my head too high? (Keep dropping your head to different levels to get a sense of where it is in relation to the floor.)
> Are my wrists bent back, with fingers pointing out to the sides?
> Are my knees at the right height to keep my lower back flat on the floor?
> Are my feet tilted correctly?
> Am I pushing my buttocks away from my head and my palms toward my feet?
> Am I pulling my shoulders toward my hips?
> Visualize your head and buttocks moving away from each other.
> Imagine that your neck is made of supple taffy, which is slowly being pulled and elongated.

WHAT IT SHOULD FEEL LIKE

When you first get into position for Dead Roach 2, your body takes a few seconds to settle into place. Then you get an "aha" moment when the stretch locks in and your body experiences its effects. During the second thirty seconds, usually you feel a dramatic stretch in the lower part of your neck.

Steeple

The Steeple stretch affects the vertebrae known as T6 and T7, which are about level with the bottom of the shoulder blades. (*T* is for *thoracic*, referring to the thorax, which is the area between the neck and abdomen.) Creating space between these two vertebrae helps release the hump in the back that most desk workers develop, along with overstretched spine muscles. Doing Steeple together with Holding a Small Globe is excellent for office workers and anyone else with a hump in the back, as well as for elderly people. I don't have a hump, but I like doing these two stretches together as a one-two punch to improve my posture.

Steeple also boosts your spleen, stomach, and diaphragm.

Sit cross-legged. Lift your chest and assume the chin-tucked head position.

> **EASY VERSION:** *If sitting cross-legged is hard for you, try sitting on a phone book, cushion, or folded blanket that raises your buttocks a few inches off the floor. If that's too difficult, start with sitting on a chair. As you become more flexible, slowly decrease the height of whatever you're sitting on until you can sit directly on the floor.*

Raise your hands above your head and press your palms together, as if you were holding a sheet of paper between your hands. As you press, push your fingertips hard toward the ceiling. Shrug your shoulders upward. Then flatten your back and lift your chest. You want your spine to be nice and straight (see Figure 6-8).

> *Although you're pushing up forcefully, you're pressing your palms together only enough to hold that piece of paper—it's a soft pressure.*
>
> ***Important:*** *don't interlock your fingers or thumbs. Your palms must touch each other. If you lock your fingers, you activate the wrong muscles and will not create the space between the vertebrae that you want.*
>
> **EASY VERSION:** *If you have weak arms or shoulders and find it tough to get your hands up there while you're pressing your palms together, start by clasping your hands on top of your head with your fingers interlocked. Then raise your arms as high as you can, straightening out your elbows.*

FIGURE 6-8

Undo your fingers only when you've extended your arms as far as you can. This trick makes raising the arms easier. You may find that it also helps the arms go higher.

As you push your fingertips upward, press your knees to the ground to anchor your body. Hold until the sixty seconds are up, or as long as you can.

TAPE LOOP

> Am I keeping my chin tucked and my head back (not tilted forward)?
> Am I pushing my fingertips toward the ceiling as forcefully as I can?
> Am I shrugging my shoulders upward?
> Am I pressing my palms together?
> Visualize your head moving toward the ceiling while your buttocks press down into the ground.

WHAT IT SHOULD FEEL LIKE

This stretch looks simple, but if your spine muscles are overstretched, you may find it rather difficult. So be patient. When you get it right, you'll feel your shoulder blades riding upward, enabling you to press your palms together more strongly. You should feel your arms really lift up out of the shoulders.

Holding a Small Globe

With this stretch, you're affecting the vertebrae known as T8 and T9 (*T* is for *thoracic*, referring to the thorax, which is the area between the neck and abdomen). Holding a Small Globe has several major benefits.

First, these two vertebrae, which lie about 2 inches below the shoulder blades, comprise the pivot point in the spine—the segment that moves the most when you walk and run. This area is subject to continuous rotation, which leads to inflammation and scarring. Runners, long-distance walkers, and basketball and soccer players must do Holding a Small Globe to keep this point flexible and healthy.

Second, most desk workers develop a hump in their back that includes this area of the spine: the front of the body is compressed and the back overstretched. Holding a Small Globe is excellent for retraining the spinal muscles to keep the back straight. It also re-creates the normal amount of space between the disks in this area. (Do it together with the Steeple stretch.) Thus, Holding a Small Globe is an essential stretch not just for office workers but for anyone with poor posture.

As a bonus, this stretch boosts the function of the liver, spleen, adrenal glands, and pancreas.

Sit on the floor with your knees bent at an angle of 90 degrees or less and your feet flat on the floor, hip width (6 to 7 inches) apart. Your knees should be no farther apart than your feet.

It's not easy to keep the feet and knees the same distance apart. Make a strong effort while keeping the intention to do this in your mind, and eventually it will happen. If you find it really difficult, do the Human Pinwheel and Buttocks Muscle stretches to release two tight muscles that are pulling your knees outward.

Assume the chin-tucked head position, lift your chest, and make your back as flat as you can. Raise one arm, straighten the elbow, and bend your wrist back, with the palm facing the ceiling and fingers pointing out to the side. Do the same with the other arm. Keep both arms in line with your spine and perfectly vertical, as if you were holding a small globe. Push hard with the *heels* of your palms (*not* your fingertips) toward the ceiling and shrug your shoulders upward. At the same time, push your feet into the floor. Hold until the sixty seconds are up (see Figures 6-9 and 6-10).

FIGURE 6-9

FIGURE 6-10
› Note straight back and arms in line with spine

People tend to raise their arches and put their weight on the outside edges of their feet, but you want to work to press the inside edges down.

EASY VERSION: *This stretch is difficult for people who are weak in the mid-back and shoulders. If you're having trouble, start with sitting in a chair. Then you can progress to sitting on the floor on a phone book or other prop that raises you several inches, and then eventually sit on the floor itself.*

Most people find at first that their arms are far forward of their spine instead of in line with it. Have someone observe you and tell you exactly where your arms are. Keeping the arms as far back as the spine can be quite difficult, so if you can't manage this, simply maintain the intention to get them there.

TAPE LOOP

> Is my head in a straight line with my spine, not tilted forward? Am I keeping a poker face?

> Are my arms in line with my spine?

> Am I pushing the arches of my feet into the floor?

> Are my knees the same distance apart as my feet, or are they flopping out to the side?

> Is my chest lifted?

> Is my back flat?

> Am I pushing the heels of my palms up and my feet into the floor at the same time?

> Am I shrugging my shoulders upward?

> Imagine that the T8 and T9 vertebrae are pulling apart and fluid is flowing in between them. (Before beginning the stretch, glance at Figure 3-1 on page 37 so you know where these vertebrae are.)

WHAT IT SHOULD FEEL LIKE

Some people have a big emotional reaction after they do this stretch. Others experience a tremendous physical release (almost like they just finished having sex), a boost in energy, or both. Still others just say, "I feel strange!" All these reactions are normal and actually great, because they mean you did it right.

Holding a Large Globe

This stretch creates space between two vertebrae, called L1 and L2, in the upper part of the lower back (*L* is for the *lumbar*, or lower-back area). Holding a Large Globe opens up the nerves that supply the thighs, so it's good for weak quadriceps and hamstrings. Doing it together with the Low Back and Hip Flexor stretches strengthens your legs and hip flexor muscles—a very cool benefit. A basketball player who did these stretches for a week before a game would be able to jump higher.

Sit on the floor and straighten your legs out in front of you as best you can.

Use a pad or cushion to raise your buttocks if that makes it easier to keep your legs straight. If you can't fully straighten out your hamstrings, that's fine—take it as far as you can tolerate.

Separate your legs as wide as you can, until you feel a strong stretch without being uncomfortable. Rotate both legs toward the center, so your knees face each other as much as possible.

Make sure the entire leg rotates, not just the foot.

Bend your feet so your toes point backward toward your body, stretching out your calves. Your goal is to tighten your quadriceps (i.e., front-of-thigh muscles) enough to bring your heels off the floor.

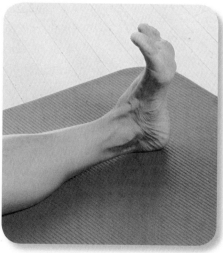

FIGURE 6-11
> Inverting foot

This is difficult for most people. If you aren't flexible enough to lift your heels off the floor, just keep that intention in mind.

Keeping the feet flexed, tilt their *outer* edges away from you. The *inner* edges come toward you. This movement is called inverting the foot; see Figure 6-11.

Raise your chest and assume the chin-tucked head position. Try as best you can to keep your back flat.

Next, position your arms. Raise one arm over your head with the elbow as straight as you can get it. Bend the wrist back so your palm faces the ceiling and your

FIGURE 6-12

fingers point out to the side. Repeat with the other arm. Shrug both shoulders upward. Your arms should not come forward but should be in line with your spine. However, they are not perfectly vertical; each arm is 3 to 4 inches away from vertical—as though you're holding up a large globe (see Figure 6-12).

Most people tend to bring their arms in front of their body, due to weak muscles in the mid- and upper back. Over time, it gets easier and easier to keep the back straight and the arms in line with the spine.

If your arms are strong enough, you can raise and position both at the same time. Muscular people in particular will find it harder to keep their elbows straight; women and thin people will find this easier.

Now you're fully in position. Hold for the rest of the sixty seconds, working to push the *heels* of your hands (*not* your fingertips) forcefully up, while keeping your knees straight, legs rotated inward, and feet bent and tilted.

TAPE LOOP

> Are my arms fully extended, in line with my spine, and with my fingers pointing out to the side?

> Am I shrugging my shoulders upward?

> Is my back flat?

> Is my chest up?

> Is my head in a straight line with my spine, not tilted forward? Am I keeping a poker face?

> Are my legs in a pigeon-toed position with my feet properly bent and tilted?

> Imagine that your L1 and L2 vertebrae are pulling apart and fluid is flowing in between them. (Before beginning the stretch, glance at Figure 3-1 on page 37 so you know where these vertebrae are.)

> Imagine your sacrum moving down toward the floor, while the top of your head moves toward the ceiling. (This isn't really going to happen, but it's a very useful mental device for pulling those vertebrae apart.)

WHAT IT SHOULD FEEL LIKE

You probably won't actually feel the L1 and L2 vertebrae pulling apart during this stretch, simply because the effort of doing it is quite distracting. But you will feel it after you finish. When you get this stretch right, you'll feel taller and more erect, and you'll have more energy in your legs and hips.

Low Back Stretch

The Low Back Stretch is one of my two favorite stretches (the other is the Hip Flexor Stretch). It works everything south of your hips, giving you a lot of bang for the buck. The focus here is the lower part of the lower back, where the bottom of the spine meets the sacrum. The sacrum is relatively fixed and stable, but the lower spine is quite mobile. Because this part of the body is greatly overused, it becomes compressed, inflamed, and heavily scarred.

This stretch decompresses the space between the L5 and S1 vertebrae (*L* is for the *lumbar*, or lower-back area, while *S* is for the *sacrum*). In other words, its goal is to separate the sacrum from the spine. Because the nerves here supply the legs and feet, the Low Back Stretch is great for sciatica and problems of the calf, ankle, and foot, such as a sprained ankle, calf pain, dropped foot, difficulty pushing off strongly during walking, plantar fasciitis, and arthritis of the toes.

The Low Back Stretch is completely different from the standard back stretch you may have learned from a physical therapist: knees to chest. That stretch doesn't address the fascia. By contrast, the Low Back Stretch stretches the entire fascial chain, from beginning to end. It's harder to perform than knees to chest, but much more effective.

Here's a little Ming experiment to show you how effective this stretch can be. Before you do it, stand up and bend forward, with your knees slightly bent. Notice the distance between the tips of your fingers and the floor. Memorize how bent your knees are with your hands at this point. Do the stretch, and then retest yourself. Most people's fingers drop 50 percent closer to the floor. I had one patient whose fingers were 8 inches above the floor before he stretched. I expected they'd drop 4 inches afterward, but when he redid the test, his fingertips actually touched the ground. He had gained the full 8 inches, and he was ecstatic.

Do not do this stretch:
> If you have active sciatica with pain shooting down your leg
> If you have acute lower-back pain greater than level 1. Wait until your pain is down to level 1. Otherwise, you may make it even worse.

For the Low Back Stretch, you need a wall. Find a spot where you can lie on your back with your legs up on the wall. You need enough room on either side to swing your legs around and up on the wall in a windshield-wiper movement.

Place a mat or blanket right up against the wall, touching it. Sit on the mat with the left side of your body against the wall. Your hip and knee should touch it. Lean back on your elbows and raise your left leg, walking it up the wall. Then walk the right leg up, swinging your torso around to face the wall. As you do this, keep your buttocks in contact with the wall or as close to it as you can. Now lie down and flatten your back so it's in complete contact with the floor while your legs rest on the wall.

If your hamstrings, calves, and lower back are tight, you won't be able to keep your buttocks against the wall and also straighten your knees. Don't feel bad—most people find either that their butts are 3 to 4 inches off the wall or that their legs are bent. If you're uncomfortable, slide your buttocks away from the wall as much as you need to.

Once my legs are against the wall, I like to rest for a minute, with my legs spread slightly apart. This position is completely relaxing and also helps me get used to having my legs elevated. This little rest isn't essential, but it makes the stretch a bit more effective. (And if you have some extra time, check the sidebar on page 108 for my Sacral Samba routine.)

Next, put your legs into position. Bend the toes of your right foot back toward your face. Keeping the foot bent in this way, tilt it so that the *inside* edge of the foot is closer to your face than the *outer* edge. (This movement is called inverting the foot; see Figure 6-11 on page 101.) The sole of the right foot is now facing to the left. Now rotate the entire right leg so that the knee and toes turn inward into a pigeon-toed position—but keep the foot bent and inverted. This is hard, but it will get easier each time you try. Finally, straighten your knee as much as you can by tensing the front of the thigh.

Straightening the knee can be uncomfortable and may cause the right side of your sacrum to come up off the floor. You'll feel a big stretch from the foot to the lower back. This is what you want! Your goal is to press your sacrum to the floor as much as possible—and at the same time, push your right heel to the ceiling. This is a real battle, and you won't be able to do it at first.

Once you have the right leg in place, position the left leg in the same way. Holding both legs in position, press both sides of your sacrum toward the floor while pushing both heels toward the ceiling. Your hips should move noticeably toward the floor. This may cause your knees to bend a little, but herein lies the challenge: try to keep your knees as straight as possible while pushing your sacrum to the ground.

FIGURE 6-13

If you're tight, this effort may be uncomfortable, but it's what produces the therapeutic effect of the stretch. Persevere!

Now assume the chin-tucked head position. Next, position your arms. Move your right arm so your hand reaches behind your head, with the arm parallel to the floor. Keeping your fingers as straight as you can, bend your right wrist so your fingers point out to the right side. Your palm pushes away from your head, toward the opposite wall. Now do the same with the left arm. Your hands and wrists should not touch the floor but should remain 1 to 2 inches above it (see Figure 6-13).

Keep your arms maximally stretched: imagine you're trying to defend the top of your head from a huge boulder that's rolling at you. Push that boulder forcefully away from your head.

If you have shoulder problems, you won't be able to do this stretch yet. Check the program for shoulder pain in Chapter 9 and use those stretches to release your shoulders first. If you don't have shoulder problems, you should be able to hold your arms in position. Some people won't be able to keep their elbows perfectly straight (I'm one of these), but that's fine.

Keep in mind that you may need twenty seconds or more just to get into position. Don't let that worry you. Hold the full stretch as long as you can, up to the full sixty seconds.

Now you are completely in position. Run your tape loop and hold for the rest of the sixty seconds or for as long as you can up to that time.

Once you become able to straighten your legs, experiment with tightening the fronts of your thighs to lift your heels away from the wall. Your goal is to have no contact between your heels and the wall. This intensifies the stretch.

Most people can't get their heels off the wall; only dancers or very flexible people can do this. But the better you can do, the greater the stretch you get.

When the sixty seconds is up, release your neck *gently*—don't let your head plop on the floor. Put your hands on your belly, let your feet go, let your knees bend a bit more, and relax. I like to stay in position for about a minute so my body can settle down, since the body needs to rest after an intense exertion.

Slowly twist to one side and sit up. Wait about thirty seconds before you stand; otherwise you might feel light-headed, since the blood quickly rushes down from your head. If you have low blood pressure, stay seated longer. Then get up on your hands and knees and push yourself up to standing.

EASY VERSION: *If getting down on the floor and up again is difficult for you, place a chair next to you, and grab onto it to pull yourself up.*

TAPE LOOP

> Are my feet flexed and tilted?
> Are my legs rotated inward so I'm pigeon-toed?
> Is my sacrum pressing down into the floor while my heels push upward?
> Are my arms pushing forcefully over my head?
> Are my wrists bent, with my fingers pointing out to the sides?
> Is my head in position—not too high? Am I keeping a poker face?
> Imagine a separation between the solid sacrum and the lowest part of the lower back. (You may not actually feel this separation at first, but visualize the space between these areas increasing. This is a psychological device; if you think about it, it'll happen.)
> Imagine that water is flowing into this space, permeating it with fluid.

WHAT IT SHOULD FEEL LIKE

After doing the Low Back Stretch for a while, you will definitely feel it creating a separation between the top of your sacrum and the bottom of your spine. You may also feel or hear little cracks and pops. These are nothing to worry about—in fact, they're a sign that your spine is decompressing. After the stretch, most people feel exhilarated, due to the release of tension and tiredness—a sense of letting go and relaxation. As you continue to do this stretch, your lower back will feel more and more stretched out.

Ming's Sacral Samba

My personal program for the Low Back Stretch involves a move I call the Sacral Samba. Since I'm basically lazy, I like to recruit other factors to do some work for me—in this case, gravity. If like me you have trouble with the Low Back Stretch, try this move—it's quite powerful.

Once you have your legs up on the wall, but before you actually begin stretching, feel underneath your sacrum with one hand to see how far off the floor your tailbone is and how far away from the wall your buttocks are. These distances are your benchmarks.

Now put your hands on your abdomen, close your eyes, and grind one side of your sacrum into the floor. Then grind the other side down. Continue alternating sides, holding for two seconds on each side and using a very slow, focused, internal movement, rather like a sinuous, seductive dance. Do this for about thirty seconds. Your goal is to grind your sacrum all the way down to the floor and bring your butt closer to the wall.

And it works! After thirty seconds, recheck the position of your sacrum and butt. Most people discover a dramatic improvement. Some shorten the distances about 50 percent, which is exactly what you want.

I like to continue sambaing for about ninety seconds to gain as much help as possible from gravity before I start the stretch. I measure both distances, samba thirty seconds, and measure how much my sacrum has dropped and how close my butt is to the wall. I samba again, measure again, and find I'm a bit closer on both counts. I samba a third time and find no changes. Then I stretch.

After the stretch, I samba once more, this time pressing both sides down and slightly harder, for about ten seconds, working to keep my knees straight and my sacrum down. Then I rest with my legs up the wall for another thirty seconds, and finally I sit up. This little program comes to about five minutes in all. But if you don't have the time, thirty seconds of sambaing is plenty.

The Fascial Stretches

L ike the spinal stretches, the fascial stretches are quite different than any other stretches you may have done. But your body will quickly become used to them. You'll develop a practical understanding of how they work and learn to adjust each one so it's maximally effective for your own body.

Say you're used to stretching your hamstrings (back-of-thigh muscles) the way everyone does: propping your leg up on a bench and leaning forward over it with a rounded back. Although you are getting some stretch in your hamstrings, you're also getting a pull in the mid- and lower back, which diffuses the stretch—it doesn't focus precisely on the hamstrings. By contrast, the Ming Method hamstring stretch feels much more profound, because it's intensely localized in the hamstrings.

After you've done the hamstring stretch a few times, you'll notice real changes. When the hamstrings are tight with their fascia all bunched up, there's excess tension in the tendons. In response, the little GPS computers shut the muscles off to prevent you from tearing something. But once a few stretching sessions have reshaped those muscles, the hamstrings start contracting properly, the GPS system kicks in and starts working right, and the muscles are stronger. Your body becomes more responsive to mental commands, you feel lighter on your feet, and you are less tired. If you're a runner, your times improve.

General Instructions for Fascial Stretching

The fascial stretches are done differently than the spinal stretches. Instead of holding for one sixty-second period, you hold for two shorter periods with a rest in between (totaling sixty seconds in all). This makes them easier to do.

Don't Overstretch

The most important rule to remember when doing fascial stretches is that *if you overstretch a muscle, you can tear it*. Keep in mind that these are very scientific, efficient stretches. You put your body in a position that gives one targeted muscle an extremely vigorous, focused stretch. To avoid injury, you absolutely must start out very slowly and gently. Here's how to keep your stretching safe:

> The muscle being stretched should not hurt. If the experience is extremely uncomfortable, especially if you feel searing or burning pain, you're pushing too hard.
> If the stretch is totally comfortable, you're not pushing hard enough.
> You want an experience that's exactly in between the previous two descriptions: definitely a little uncomfortable, but not really painful.
> When you put your body in the preparatory position for a stretch, never take any of the movements (e.g., turning your head, rotating your torso, pulling your shoulder blades together) to the limit. Go

only to 80 percent of your ability, and save some flexibility for the stretch itself. If you try to push farther a muscle that's already at its max, you may injure yourself.

My advice is: *always err on the side of caution.* Take each stretch just to the point where you're slightly uncomfortable and hold right there, gently, for the remainder of your stretch time. Then *stop* and save any further effort for the next day. Each day, increase the stretch ever so slightly—in increments so small that they're barely perceptible. Ride the line between slightly uncomfortable and too easy, and you'll be in just the right place.

Advanced practitioners of yoga and Pilates, gymnasts, professional dancers, and others whose disciplines create an understanding of the dynamics of stretching can start out somewhat more aggressively. But remember even advanced practitioners can injure themselves if they stretch too forcefully.

Never Stretch When You're Cold

Another general rule is to *never stretch an area that's cold.* Before stretching, you need to warm up and get your blood flowing. The body contains miles of tiny arteries, most of which stay closed unless you have moved enough to open them up and fill them with blood. After just a few minutes of movement, these baby blood vessels will open. The muscles they bring blood to grow warm and loosen up, allowing all that water you're drinking to get into the fascia. That's why the best time to stretch is after a workout, when all these arteries are open. Be sure to warm up the specific part of the body you plan to stretch.

If you don't do regular workouts, just do some very simple movements:

> Windmill your arms.
> Rotate your torso.
> Do neck rolls.
> Touch your toes (bending forward as far as you can comfortably).
> Make circles with your knees.

> Jog slowly in place for thirty seconds. (If you can't jog, hold on to a chair and march in place.)
> Do calf raises. (Holding onto a chair, come up onto the balls of your feet and then lower your heels slowly to the floor.)

All you need are 10 to 15 rhythmic repetitions on each side, just to loosen yourself up—a total of two minutes of nonstop movement. The key is that *you must sweat slightly*. If you don't break a sweat, you're not warmed up enough, and you need to repeat a couple of the warm-up movements for an extra minute or so.

Timing the Stretches

You don't need to hold fascial stretches for an uninterrupted sixty-second period. For most people, this would be quite difficult. So you break each fascial stretch into two sections, with a rest in between. After the rest, in the second part of the stretch, you can go farther.

Here's the basic timing for all but two of the stretches in this chapter:

> Hold for twenty seconds.
> Rest for ten seconds.
> Hold for thirty seconds.

The first twenty seconds is essentially a warm-up for the following thirty-second hold. Most people need five to ten seconds just to get into position, so don't worry if the first hold doesn't seem to be doing much. On the second hold, you'll get into position much faster, and—here's the key—you should make a greater effort. The thirty-second hold does the majority of the work. During this part, strive for an additional 5 percent of stretch beyond what you got in the first part. This requires a mental focus on expecting and working toward that small extra increment of movement. Even after you've stretched as much as you can, you can always go another 1 percent—so strive for that as well. If you don't challenge yourself to your end point, you won't get the full benefit. Remember the Kaizen principle of continuous small improvements that I described in Chapter 3? It works here, too. Keep asking, is it still releasing? Just remember you are *listening* to your body, *not* trying to force it. When it says no, that's where you must stop.

At the beginning, put a clock with a second hand in front of you to time your stretch-rest-stretch intervals. After a while, you won't need it because you'll know how long twenty seconds is. Besides, with the fascial stretches, these time periods are basically just guidelines. The actual time you need depends on how well hydrated you are and the amount of injury and scarring in the part of the body you're stretching. If your fascia is unhealthy, you need a longer hold to stretch it enough to get a good release. As you come to understand how the stretches work, you might decide to add a few extra seconds to your hold time, but always remember to be *gentle* and *not force* your tissue beyond that sense of slight discomfort. As your fascia gets healthier, your hold times can be shorter. You'll be able to get into position immediately, so you can hold a few seconds less.

As you hold, there will be a moment when you suddenly feel the muscle fibers separating as the muscle opens and releases. When this happens, hold right there as long as you still feel this opening—being gentle yet firm at the same time. When the sensation of opening stops, let go. The optimal timing is slightly different for everyone. Once again, you must listen to your body—it will tell you. You might hold for thirty seconds, twenty-eight, or forty. What's important is to consciously use the second hold period for the main therapeutic work.

Special Note for Elderly People

Since older people can be quite dehydrated, with tight, inflexible tissues, they must be extra careful. Be *very* gentle, and be sure not to stretch so hard that it causes a searing or burning sensation.

More Tips

> Unless the programs in Chapter 9 direct otherwise, do the fascial stretches in order from the top of the body downward. This instruction applies particularly to the stretches I recommend in Chapter 8 to help you do the strengthening exercises correctly.

〉 Take your shoes off before stretching.

〉 Since the fascial stretches aren't used to release spinal compression, there's no special benefit to doing them just before bed. You can do them at any time of the day.

〉 It's essential to make sure that all the components of each stretch are in place. The positions of the head, feet, hands, and so on lock down specific parts of the fascial chain. If any part of this chain isn't held in tension, you won't properly stretch the particular fascia you're focusing on.

〉 Relax your face. Clenching the jaw actually distracts from your ability to focus on the area being stretched. The only muscles that should be tight are the ones you're contracting to hold the position.

〉 The instruction to keep the head in neutral position is not the same as chin-tucking the head. It simply means that the chin is level—not tilted up or down—and the head itself is not tilted to either the right or the left.

〉 Since everyone's body is different, you need to play around slightly with each stretch to make it work for you. I explain in the instructions how to make small adjustments to modify the stretch for your unique body. I also tell you what the stretch should feel like, and you can use that as a guide for experimenting. Remember, you will *not* get this feeling the first time you do a stretch. Just keep adjusting until you do.

〉 Chapter 2 discussed the plasticity of the fascia—its ability to be reshaped. An excellent mental device to use with all the fascial stretches is to imagine that the muscle you're focusing on is a piece of taffy that's being gently pulled and lengthened.

〉 For the sake of simplicity, the instructions in this chapter all describe doing the stretches on the right side. However, you should always do a fascial stretch on both sides of the body, even if one side is tighter than the other. There are two reasons for this. First, stretching the more flexible side first prepares your body mentally for stretching the other side, giving you confidence that the stretch is achievable on the tight side. Second, the nonactive side of the body learns the ropes from the side that's stretching and can release more when its turn comes. So stretching the flexible side first actually makes it easier to stretch the tight side.

Side-of-Neck Stretch

Along each side of your neck runs a set of three broad, thin muscles called the scalenes, whose job is to stabilize the head on the neck. Starting at the middle of the back of the neck, running under the back of the jaw, and ending below the collarbone in front, these muscles are involved in many shoulder, arm, wrist, and finger problems. In fact, what doctors often misdiagnose as carpal tunnel syndrome or tennis elbow actually originates from short, tight scalenes compressing the nerves that go to the arm. The Side-of-Neck Stretch is thus helpful for a wide range of painful conditions and really great for computer users.

You can do this stretch either seated or standing. Hold your right arm out along your side, about 15 inches away from your hip. Bend the wrist backward and rotate the arm so the inside crease of your elbow faces up and away from your body.

Raise your chest, and rotate your head about 2 inches to the left. Maintain the rotation while you *tilt* your head about 2 inches to the left. Jut your jaw forward, and at the same time press your right shoulder and arm downward, away from your chin. Hold for twenty seconds, relax for ten seconds, and then hold for thirty seconds (see Figure 7-1).

Jutting out the jaw is essential for getting results.

Caution: *these muscles are thin and delicate, so be careful. The twenty-second hold should be very gentle. The thirty-second hold can be a little more intense. If you overstretch, you can tear the fascia in your neck, which will give you many days of pain.*

Repeat the entire stretch on the left side.

FIGURE 7-1

TAPE LOOP

> Is my arm rotated so that the inside of the elbow faces away from my body?
> Am I jutting my jaw out?
> Am I pressing my shoulder away from my chin?
> Imagine the wide, thin muscles at the side of the neck pulling apart, as though you were pulling a sheet of plastic wrap taut over a bowl of food.

WHAT IT SHOULD FEEL LIKE

You should *not* get a tearing or burning sensation from this stretch. Instead, you should have a more subtle feeling that a broad, thin band is being pulled from underneath the jaw to the base of the neck.

Front-of-Shoulder Stretch

This stretch targets the muscle at the front of the shoulder (coracobrachialis) that is primarily responsible for raising the arm forward. The Front-of-Shoulder Stretch is helpful for frozen shoulder and rotator cuff injuries.

Sit on the edge of a chair with your feet flat on the floor and wider than shoulder-width apart. Place your hands on the outsides of your thighs, with your thumbs on top and your fingers gripping the sides of your thighs. Lean forward. Your elbows will come behind your back.

Slowly drive the point of your right shoulder toward an imaginary spot on the floor midway between your feet. When you feel a good stretch at the front of your right shoulder, rotate your torso to the left.

Do not just turn your head—make sure your entire torso *turns.*

With your torso turned to the left, rotate your head to the left and drop your chin to touch your collarbone at the upper left side of your chest. Use your right hand pressing into your thigh to rotate your torso even more. Hold for twenty seconds (see Figure 7-2).

Rotating your head is not enough here—you must also press your chin down. This is not the same as the chin-tucked head position, where you keep your chin in a neutral position. For the Front-of-Shoulder Stretch, you must actually drop your chin.

Don't let your right elbow come forward—keep it no farther than 3 inches away from your side.

After releasing the first hold, sit back up and relax, letting your breathing come back to normal. Now go back into the stretch and hold for thirty seconds.

Repeat the entire stretch on the left side.

FIGURE 7-2

TAPE LOOP

> Is my chin against my collarbone on the side opposite the side I'm stretching?
> Am I actively pressing my shoulder down between my feet?
> Imagine a strap running diagonally from the front of the shoulder down past the armpit. The strap slowly lengthens as you stretch.

WHAT IT SHOULD FEEL LIKE

When you do this stretch correctly, you can feel the muscle like a strap being pulled diagonally across the front of your shoulder, from the end of the collarbone toward the armpit.

Deep Shoulder Stretches

The four deep muscles that form the rotator cuff are responsible for turning the arm inward and outward, and also for fine-tuning the action of raising the arm. To fully release these muscles, you need two stretches.

The first one works on the muscles that rotate the arm inward; the second one affects the muscles that rotate it outward. These stretches relieve shoulder problems, including frozen shoulder.

Deep Shoulder Stretch 1

Lie facedown on the floor. Separate your knees and bend them so your feet come up off the floor. Gently press the soles of your feet together, with just the amount of pressure you'd need to hold a piece of paper between them. Place your left hand in push-up position, and turn your head to the right. Extend your right arm out at a 90-degree angle to your torso. Bend your right elbow at a 90-degree angle, and bend your wrist back.

If you're flexible, you may need to place a small rolled towel under your wrist (and under your elbow, too). You can also try pushing with your left hand to lift the left side of your chest from the floor. Both actions intensify the stretch.

If you aren't flexible, you may want to put a pillow under your chest to decrease the amount of stretch.

Press your left hand into the floor to slide your torso about 1 inch to the left. Your right elbow does not move as you do this, except that the flesh underneath it rolls slightly. This action creates space in the shoulder joint. Now press your pelvis and your right shoulder into the floor. Hold for twenty seconds, rest for ten seconds, and then hold for another thirty seconds (see Figure 7-3).

Sliding the torso to the left is a subtle movement, but you should be able to feel it create an opening deep inside your shoulder joint.

Get out of position slowly by using your fingers to walk the right hand in a clockwise direction.

Repeat on the left side.

FIGURE 7-3

TAPE LOOP

⟩ Are my feet pressed together?
⟩ Is my wrist bent back?
⟩ Is my head turned to the right?
⟩ Are my right shoulder and my pelvis pressing into the floor?

WHAT IT SHOULD FEEL LIKE

You should feel this stretch like a twist occurring deep inside the shoulder. This is what I call a bright stretch—it causes a discomfort like someone shining a light in your eyes. However, this feeling usually decreases during the thirty-second hold. If you have shoulder problems, you may have a creaky feeling as you come out of position. That's because it feels odd to stretch muscles you never stretched before.

Deep Shoulder Stretch 2

Stand with your back against a wall. Your heels should be about 6 inches away from the wall, less if you're short or thin. Put your right hand behind your back at waist level, with the palm flat against the wall.

There's a little shelf in your lower back where your hand naturally fits. Ideally your palm is right at the center of your spine. But if you can't get it this far, that's OK. Your hand may reach only to the middle of the right side of your back. As you release the rotator cuff muscles, you'll be able to reach farther. But if you're very flexible, you may need to reach your hand past your spine to the left side of your back.

With your chin in neutral position, turn your head as far as you can to the right. Strongly lift your chest. Step 1 inch to the left without changing the position of your hand on the wall. This action creates space in the shoulder joint.

The shift to the left is subtle. You may need to move only ½ inch to feel the space open up in your shoulder.

Once you feel that space open up, press your right hand against the wall and press your right shoulder backward into the wall. Hold for twenty seconds, rest for ten seconds, and then hold for another thirty seconds (see Figure 7-4).

As soon as you press your shoulder into the wall, your shoulder blade pops up. Your goal is to keep it down, and that's hard to do. The trick is to do a "shoulder samba," gently pressing the palm and then the shoulder into the wall in turn, working to get the shoulder blade to drop. This is a slow, rhythmic movement—see the instructions for the Sit Bone Samba on page 148 and the Sacral Samba on page 108. As you samba, do a subtle side-to-side movement of your whole body, with your feet staying in place. Just ½ inch in each direction really helps open up the shoulder.

To get out of position, walk your fingers to the right across the wall and then gently bring your arm down, straighten it, and shake it out. *Do not* explode out of the stretch.

Getting out of position can be uncomfortable: the shoulder feels creaky like a door hinge that needs oil. This is normal; it means you've done the stretch well!

Repeat on the left side.

FIGURE 7-4

TAPE LOOP
> Is my chest lifted?
> Is my head turned as far to the right as it can go?
> Is my shoulder pressing backward into the wall?

WHAT IT SHOULD FEEL LIKE

This is a deep, bright stretch like the previous inward rotation stretch; it's somewhat uncomfortable, as if your shoulder were a creaky door hinge slowly being opened. Afterward, your arm may feel odd, so it's good to shake it out.

Shrug Muscle Stretch

The "shrug" muscle is the trapezius, which runs all the way from the lower back out to the shoulder and up to the base of the skull. This stretch releases the upper part of the trapezius, which shrugs your shoulder—and contracts into a knot when you're tense. The Shrug Muscle Stretch is excellent to relieve stress. It helps people who suffer from migraines that start at the bottom of the neck and wrap over the back of the head and down to the eyebrows. It's also good for what people call a stiff neck but which really is a tight trapezius.

FIGURE 7-5

You can do this stretch seated or standing. Hold your right arm about 5 inches out from your hip, keeping your elbow straight, and bend your wrist back. Drop your chin to your chest. Rotate your head to the right about 30 degrees and then maintain the rotation while you tilt your head to the left about 80 percent of the distance it can go. Press your right shoulder down hard, away from your ear. Hold for twenty seconds, rest for ten seconds, and then hold again for thirty seconds (see Figure 7-5).

Important: *make sure your elbow is straight and your wrist bent back. Push forcefully toward the floor with the heel of your palm.*

If you feel a burning sensation, you're pushing too hard—but you shouldn't be comfortable, either.

Repeat on the left side.

TAPE LOOP

> Is my head rotated to the right?
> Is my head tilted to the left?
> Is my wrist bent back?
> Is my elbow straight?
> Am I pressing my shoulder down as hard as I can?

WHAT IT SHOULD FEEL LIKE

You will feel this stretch from the back of your head to the outer edge of your shoulder, as though a thick cord is elongating.

Mid-Back Stretch

etween your spine and the inner edge of your shoulder blade lies a muscle called the rhomboid, which is responsible for pain that hits right in the middle of your back. In people who spend a lot of time leaning over a desk or anyone with poor posture (unfortunately, that's most of us), the rhomboid is always over-stretched and full of scar tissue. This is in con-trast to most of the other muscles we stretch, which are *contracted* and full of scar tissue.

You need to stretch the rhomboid to break up the scarring, but you want to get it out of its weak, overstretched state as soon as possible. The program in Chapter 8 is specifically designed to strengthen the entire back of the body, including the rhomboid. But if you have the time, it's a good idea to do the Chest Muscle and Biceps stretches in addition to the Mid-Back Stretch until you're ready to start the strengthening program. These two stretches have the extra benefit of strength-ening the rhomboid (see pages 127 and 129).

The Mid-Back Stretch is good for frozen shoulder and for pain in the middle of the back, which many people are prone to have, such as office workers, massage therapists, draftsmen, dentists, and hair stylists.

Sit on the edge of a chair. Swing your right arm in front of you and over to the left as far as you can. Bend your right wrist back so your fingers point toward the floor as much as possible. Keep your elbow as straight as you can. Turn your head to the right as far as you can. Lift your chest, and keep your head in neutral position.

Bring your left arm under your right arm, and take hold of your right upper arm with your left hand. Use your left hand to pull your right shoulder or arm to the left. Contract your right chest muscle. As you do this, imagine that you're turning your torso very slightly to the right. Now focus your mind on sliding your right shoulder blade across your back, toward your right side. Hold for twenty seconds, rest for ten seconds, and then hold again for thirty sec-onds (see Figure 7-6).

FIGURE 7-6

If you're flexible, hold on to your right shoulder with your left hand.
The mental device of imagining that you are turning the torso slightly
to the right actually makes a huge difference in the amount of stretch you
get. Be sure, in any case, not to turn your torso to the left as you pull your
right arm to the left.

Repeat on the left side.

TAPE LOOP

> Is my chest lifted?
> Is my head rotated to the right?
> Am I mentally trying to turn my torso slightly to the right?
> Am I contracting my right chest muscle?
> Is my elbow as straight as I can get it and my wrist bent back?
> Imagine a piece of plastic wrap spreading between your spine and the inner edge of your shoulder blade.

WHAT IT SHOULD FEEL LIKE

You feel this 4-inch-wide muscle spreading out between your spine and the inner edge of your shoulder blade as the shoulder blade slides to the right. This broad stretch feels like a piece of plastic wrap spreading across your back, a very nice sensation.

Broad Back Stretch

This stretch releases the "lat," or latissimus dorsi, which is the big triangular muscle that begins at the bottom of the spine and runs to the upper arm bone, just below the armpit. Because the muscle is so large, this is an extremely powerful stretch. It significantly increases your shoulder mobility and also relieves lower-back and hip pain, since the muscle attaches to the lower spine and sacrum—a prime example of how the different parts of the body are connected.

Sit on your heels, and then bend forward over your knees, which should be about 4 inches apart. Turn your head to the right. Place your left hand in push-up position. Stretch your right arm over your head, rotate it outward as far as you can, and bend the wrist backward. Push the right arm forward, keeping the elbow as straight as possible.

Now shift the right side of your rib cage to the right by contracting the left side of your torso. Use your left arm to help push your right ribs to the right. Imagine the ribs on the right side opening, as though you were pulling the string of a bow. Hump your back like a turtle, straighten the right arm even more, and then stretch it forward again. Hold for twenty seconds, rest for ten seconds, and then hold again for thirty seconds (see Figure 7-7).

FIGURE 7-7

Humping your back helps the lat stretch farther.

Important: *if you get a burning sensation, relax and start again more slowly. You should feel less discomfort during the thirty-second hold, which means the muscle is slowly opening. During this hold, you can go for the extra 5 percent release.*

Repeat on the left side.

TAPE LOOP

> Is my head rotated to the right?
> Is my right arm rotated outward as far as possible, with the elbow straight and the wrist bent back?
> Is my left arm pushing to the right?
> Am I pushing the right arm strongly forward?
> Imagine a piece of plastic wrap spreading across your back.

WHAT IT SHOULD FEEL LIKE

You feel a very intense stretch along the side of your torso, from the armpit to the hips. The muscle covers a wide area, so when it's stretched you feel as though a piece of plastic wrap is spreading across your back.

Chest Muscle Stretch

This stretch affects the large muscle that covers the top front of the chest, from the breastbone to the front of the shoulder (pectoralis major). The Chest Muscle Stretch is critical for treating any kind of shoulder problem. It's also great for office workers, whose chest muscles are usually shortened by the hours spent leaning over a desk.

If you have a frozen shoulder, put a pillow beneath your chest and stretch extremely gently at the beginning. **Caution:** it's easy to tear this muscle if you overstretch, so stay alert!

Lie facedown. Place your left palm on the floor by your shoulder in push-up position. Turn your head to the left. Keep it off the floor at a comfortable level, without bending your neck. Extend your right arm out to the side at shoulder level, then slide it 3 to 5 inches above your shoulder. To determine the correct position for you, try moving the arm 3 inches up, then 4 inches, then 5 inches. Use the position in which you feel the maximum stretch.

Now bend the right wrist back and rotate the arm backward as much as you can so that your little finger comes toward the floor. Push the heel of your palm very hard away from your body.

Pushing the palm away really hard is essential: this action creates space in the shoulder joint.

Rotate your hips so that you're lying on your right hip. Bend your knees 90 degrees to the right. Your thighs are in a straight line with your torso, and your calves are perpendicular to your thighs. Your feet point behind you.

Now contract your buttocks to push your pelvis forward. Gently but firmly press your right shoulder into the floor. Contract your back muscles to squeeze your right shoulder blade toward your spine. Use your left hand pushing into the floor to control the intensity of the stretch by rotating your body to the right. Hold for twenty seconds, rest for ten seconds, and hold for another thirty seconds (see Figure 7-8).

Squeezing the shoulder blade toward the spine is the key action that triggers Sherrington's law (see Chapter 3). A side benefit is that this contraction strengthens the rhomboid, a muscle in the middle of the back that tends to be chronically overstretched and weak (see page 123).

FIGURE 7-8

Your left hand determines the range of the stretch by rotating the torso. If your chest muscle is tight, you won't want to do this rotation at all. If you're flexible, you can carefully use your left hand to increase the intensity of the stretch.

Pressing the right shoulder into the floor is an essential part of this stretch, because this action really stretches the muscle.

Repeat on the left side.

TAPE LOOP

> Am I keeping my right arm rotated and pushing the palm forcefully away from my body?
> Am I pushing my right shoulder into the floor?
> Am I squeezing my right shoulder blade toward my spine?
> Are my buttocks contracted?
> Imagine that you're pulling the joint apart, as the upper arm bone moves out of the shoulder.
> Visualize the chest muscle being gently stretched out and remaining elongated.

WHAT IT SHOULD FEEL LIKE

You should feel this stretch in your chest right below your collarbone and out to the front of the shoulder. Some people feel it all the way from the breastbone to the shoulder. If you don't feel anything, push your left hand into the floor to rotate your body more to the right.

Biceps Stretch

The biceps is the well-known muscle that pops up on the inside of the upper arm when you bend your elbow. The Biceps Stretch helps with a range of problems: shoulder pain (frozen shoulder in particular), rotator cuff problems, carpal tunnel syndrome, tennis elbow, and golfer's elbow. As an added benefit, doing this stretch strengthens the always weak and overstretched mid-back (rhomboid) muscle (see page 123).

For this stretch you need a stable chair (one that doesn't roll) and a low table. You must be able to sit on the chair and rest your arms behind you on the table with the backs of your hands lying flat. Depending on your height, the heights of the chair and table, and how tight your shoulders are, you can modify your position to get the right amount of stretch. For example, if the chair is too low, sit on a cushion. If the table is too high and you get a lot of tension in your biceps, lean forward to reduce it. You can adjust this stretch in many ways to get it right for you.

Sit in the chair with your feet flat on the floor, a comfortable distance apart. Put both arms on the table behind you, with the backs of your hands facing down on the table. Your hands should be slightly more than shoulder width apart.

Pull both shoulders backward, and lift your chest. Walk your feet slightly to the left to help you rotate your torso to the left until you feel some tension, but leave a little slack for the stretch itself. Consciously straighten your right elbow; this contracts the triceps on the other side of your upper arm and kicks in Sherrington's law. Bend your right wrist up and bring the fingers and thumb to touch each other in a point, making a tulip shape with the hand. Your left hand can stay flat on the table.

Your goal is to keep the back of your right hand off the table. Some people can't do this, but it's your intention.

Tilt your head to the left, and keeping it tilted, rotate your head to the left and drop your chin to touch your left collarbone. Hold for twenty seconds, rest for ten seconds, and then hold for another thirty seconds (see Figure 7-9).

Rotate your head enough to stretch the right side of your neck.
The tendency is to let the shoulders drop forward, but you want instead to squeeze the shoulder blades together, while keeping your chest lifted.

This stretch can be quite intense, so start out extremely gently. The biceps is a small muscle, and you can easily tear it. Increase the tension slowly until you feel the magical moment of maximum tension. If the stretch is painful and you feel a burning sensation, you're being too aggressive! Back off immediately to avoid an overstretch injury.

Repeat on the left side.

FIGURE 7-9

TAPE LOOP

> Most important: Is my wrist bent?
> Are my fingers pointed in a tulip shape?
> Am I strongly contracting my triceps to hold my elbow straight?
> Are my shoulders pulled back?
> Is my torso rotated to the left?
> Is my head tilted and rotated to the left?
> Is my chin pointed at (or touching) my collarbone?
> Imagine there's an olive on your spine between your shoulder blades. Squeeze that olive as hard as you can to get the oil out of it.

WHAT IT SHOULD FEEL LIKE

You feel the muscle like a strap or band being pulled, extending from the top front of your shoulder to your elbow. Depending on where the tight areas are—and on how tight the other arm and shoulder muscles are—people feel this stretch most strongly in different places: in front of the shoulder, in the middle of the upper arm, near the elbow, or all the way to the wrist.

Triceps Stretch

The triceps is the muscle that runs along the back of the upper arm from the elbow to the back of the shoulder. This stretch is for shoulder problems, elbow problems, and wrist and hand problems.

Lean the right side of your body against a wall. Raise your right arm as high as possible. Your goal is to have that arm be vertical, but if you can't, get it as close to vertical as you can. With both your arm and your ribs touching the wall, move your body toward the wall to minimize the space between the wall and your armpit. Try to press your armpit flat against the wall.

Now bend your right elbow so your hand goes behind your head, as though you're going to scratch the bottom of your neck, or if you're flexible, the upper part of your back. Your fingers are straight and point toward the floor. Keep your head in neutral position.

If you're very flexible and your arm is completely vertical, you may need to move your head slightly forward to get it out of the way.

Here's a trick to enhance this stretch: while the right arm is still straight up along the wall, raise up onto your toes. Then as you bend your elbow, lower your heels to the floor, using the downward movement of your body to increase the opening of the armpit.

Now rotate your right wrist to your right. This makes the little finger move away from your back (see Figure 7-10). Then rotate the wrist to the left, so the thumb moves away from your back (see Figure 7-11). Here you do some self-diagnosis: decide which of these two motions is more difficult. That's the one you hold, because it targets the tightest part of the muscle.

The last step is to consciously tense the right biceps (the muscle on the inside of the upper arm) as strongly as you can. This action triggers Sherrington's law to release the triceps. Hold for twenty seconds, rest for ten seconds, and then hold for another thirty seconds.

Repeat on the left side.

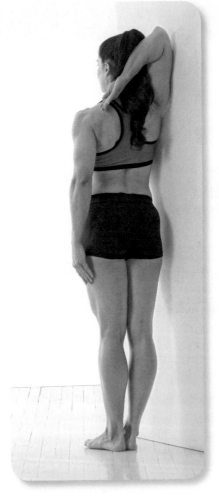

FIGURE 7-11
> Wrist rotated to left

FIGURE 7-10
> Wrist rotated to right

TAPE LOOP

> Is my head in as neutral a position as possible?
> Is my wrist rotated all the way in the direction I chose?
> Am I strongly tensing my biceps?
> Imagine the muscle being pulled apart like taffy along the back of your upper arm.

WHAT IT SHOULD FEEL LIKE

When you're doing the stretch correctly, you feel as if a rope is being pulled along the back of your upper arm, from the armpit to the elbow.

Wrist and Forearm Stretches

These two stretches target the muscles that bend the wrist forward and backward, open and close the fingers, and enable you to make a fist. These primary movers of the hands actually start at the elbow and run down the arms, and the stretches affect their entire length. The Wrist and Forearm Stretches are excellent for arthritic fingers and carpal tunnel syndrome. Use them for any problems with power and dexterity in your fingers and also for elbow problems. Baby boomers, elderly people, and anyone who types a lot absolutely must do them. These stretches also help you extend your arms backward when doing the spinal stretches.

Caution: if you have active carpal tunnel syndrome and your tissue is very inflamed, *do not* do these stretches until the inflammation has subsided. After that, they will be very effective.

1. Inside-of-Forearm Stretch

Stand facing a table or counter that comes to about hip level. Don't use a soft surface like a sofa or bed, but put a thin layer of padding such as a soft towel or a blanket on the table or counter.

Place your palms on the table with the tips of your fingers pointing toward you. Keep your elbows straight, and spread your fingers wide like a web. Slowly exert downward pressure into your palms, and imagine the palms flattening down onto the table. If you can't get the heels of the palms to touch the table, just take it to your point of tolerance.

Once you reach your point of maximal stretch, straighten out the fingers as strongly as you can, while imagining that you're trying to lift the fingertips off the table. Most people won't be able to do this, but what's important is focusing on the *intention* to do so, for this triggers Sherrington's law and releases the muscles on the insides of the forearms. Hold for twenty seconds, rest for ten seconds, and then hold for another thirty seconds (see Figure 7-12).

Notice how straight each finger is. If an individual finger bends instead of flattening, actively work to press it down. If the finger resists and won't flatten out, release the other hand and use it to press that finger into place.

You can also do this stretch on all fours on the floor.

FIGURE 7-12

TAPE LOOP

❯ Are my elbows straight?

❯ Am I pressing the heels of my palms down?

❯ Are all my fingers as flat as I can get them?

❯ Am I working to lift the tips of my fingers off the table?

❯ Imagine putting a drop of ink on a tissue and watching it spread. Visualize your fingers spreading out in the same way.

WHAT IT SHOULD FEEL LIKE

You should feel a profound, intense stretch along the insides of your forearms, from the elbows to the wrists, and also in your wrists and palms.

2. Outside-of-Forearm Stretch

This time, place the *backs* of your hands on the table, with your fingers pointing toward you. This is uncomfortable, so make sure you use cushioning. Keep your elbows straight. Press down, bending the wrists more and more as you increase the pressure *very gently*. Your goal is to get the entire backs of the hands, from the wrists to the fingertips, to touch the table. If you can't do this, go as far as you can.

Now pinch the fingers and thumb of each hand together to make little bowls—or, as I like to say, double tulips. This action kicks in Sherrington's law.

Finally, actively bend your wrists even farther, working to get your knuckles off the table. This is really difficult, but even if you can't actually do it, have that intention in mind. Hold for twenty seconds, rest for ten seconds, and then hold another thirty seconds (see Figure 7-13).

You can also do this stretch on all fours on the floor.

FIGURE 7-13

TAPE LOOP

> Are my elbows straight?
> Am I actively pinching my fingers into double tulips?
> Am I working to get my knuckles off the table?

WHAT IT SHOULD FEEL LIKE

You should feel a strong stretch along the outsides of your forearms from the elbows down to the wrists. Sometimes people get a cramp on the inside of the forearm. If this happens, just relax for a few seconds and then go back into position.

Hip Flexor Stretch

The Hip Flexor Stretch is one of my two favorites (the other is the Low Back Stretch). Objectively, this is also one of the most important of all stretches. The very deep muscle it affects, the psoas, begins at the front of the spine in the lower back and runs down through the pelvis all the way to the hip joint. The Hip Flexor Stretch is key for basic health because the psoas is attached to every single organ in the abdomen and pelvis. When the psoas is contracted, these organs become constricted. When it's stretched, the organs benefit from increased circulation and stronger nerve impulses, which make them healthier.

A tight psoas exerts a downward and forward pull on the lower spine—a major but underrated cause of lower-back pain. Because back pain affects the back of the body, no one thinks of stretching the front. Most doctors will tell you to relieve lower-back pain by stretching your hamstrings and strengthening your abdominal muscles. I beg to differ: the key muscle to treat is the hip flexor. This is another example of how the fascia connects seemingly unrelated parts of the body.

Anyone who spends a lot of time sitting should do the Hip Flexor Stretch, because sitting shortens the psoas and thereby the area from the bottom of the spine to the groin. This stretch decompresses the spine and prevents you from developing the bent-forward posture seen in so many elderly people. Others who should do it include:

> Cyclists, who bend forward over their handlebars
> Kicking athletes, such as soccer players and martial artists, who develop a lot of scarring in the psoas from forward kicks
> Anyone with a hamstring pull—a common injury in baseball and basketball (in my experience, a tight psoas creates a weakness in the hamstrings that leaves them vulnerable to pulls)

Two additional reasons why the Hip Flexor Stretch is so powerful: it relieves constipation, and it has a wonderful strengthening effect on the buttocks, helping correct poor posture.

Caution: to avoid injuring your knees, you must do the Hip Flexor Stretch on a soft surface that has more padding than just a carpet or mat. Put a pillow or foam pad on top of the carpet and place your knee on that.

Kneel on your right knee and bring your left leg in front of you, with the left foot flat on the floor and left knee bent 90 degrees. You can prop your right foot up on the toes or leave the top of the foot on the floor. Since the right heel must angle out to the side, put the foot in the position that facilitates keeping the right ankle slightly to the outside of the right knee.

Hold both arms out in front of you, with the elbows straight and the inside crease of the elbows facing up. Bend your wrists so your palms face away from you, with your fingertips pointing toward the floor.

Tilt your entire torso to the *left*, bowing your ribs out to the right. Tilt to 80 percent of your ability to stretch that right side. Now maintain the tilt while *rotating* your torso to the *right*, again to 80 percent of your range.

> *It's tricky to tilt your torso in one direction and then maintain that tilt while you rotate the torso in the opposite direction. Most people lose the tilt when they rotate to the other side, so remember to stay tilted. You'll probably need a couple of sessions to get the hang of doing both actions at the same time.*

Hold this position and slowly lower your left hand to your left thigh, with the elbow hanging off the side. Lift your chest, and then chin-tuck your head.

> *Make sure the left elbow hangs loose off the side of the thigh—don't lock it down on the thigh. That arm should stay relaxed.*

Clench your buttocks forcefully to press your *right* hip forward. Make sure that your back does not arch: contract your abdominal muscles to prevent this. Now think in your mind that you're dragging your right knee straight in front of you, and contract the muscles you would use to do this. Press down with your right foot as you drag.

> *Dragging the right knee is a mental device. The knee doesn't actually move, but if you do this action in your mind, the appropriate muscles will contract and you'll give the psoas a great stretch, as though a crease in the front of your hip is opening up. Make sure you clench your buttocks like you were clenching a fist. This action is what triggers Sherrington's law and gives the psoas the message to let go. However, the act of clenching the buttocks tends to make people arch their backs, so make sure you contract your abdominals to avoid this.*

As you drag your right knee, you feel an end point beyond which your body can't stretch. When you reach that point, hold your buttocks firmly contracted for the rest of the twenty-second hold. Relax for ten seconds; then go back into position and hold for another thirty seconds (see Figures 7-14 and 7-15).

FIGURE 7-14

FIGURE 7-15

If you're fairly flexible and feel you can stretch farther, bend your left knee slightly to bring your body forward.

Even when you feel you've contracted your buttocks maximally, there's always another 1 percent to go. During the thirty-second stretch, even though you feel you've achieved your extra 5 percent, contract your buttocks just a little bit harder. You'll feel the crease in the front of your hip open that much more. This is the goal of the entire stretch.

Caution: *don't try for the additional 1 percent until you've done the stretch for a week and have already experienced some opening in your hip.*

EASY VERSION: *Use two chairs, one on either side. Place the palm of each hand on the seat of a chair. You still rotate and tilt the torso and tuck the chin.*

Repeat the stretch on the left side.

TAPE LOOP

> Is my rear heel angled out past my knee?

> Most important: are my buttocks firmly clenched?

> Are my abdominals tensed so my lower back isn't arched?

> Is my head in the chin-tuck position?

> Is my chest lifted?

> Is my torso still tilted to the left and rotated to the right?

> Imagine the front of your hip opening wide, out of a creased and bent position, as the tissue there stretches like a piece of taffy being pulled.

WHAT IT SHOULD FEEL LIKE

The opening in the crease of the hip is a striking feeling, almost as if you're bending the crease outward. It's distinct and unmistakable, a clear "aha" moment like a lightbulb suddenly turned on.

I love this stretch because I feel so tall afterward. When you stand up and walk around, you'll feel taller and your gait will be much freer. Remember, though, that most people don't get these effects until the third or fourth time they do the stretch. So don't be discouraged!

Quad Stretches

The four muscles that run down the front of the thigh are called the quadriceps. If they're tight, they pull the knee up, causing knee problems. Tight quads also pull the pelvis downward, tilting the torso forward and causing lower-back problems. To release the four quads, you need two stretches. The first is a general release that affects all of them; it's excellent for any problems with the knee or kneecap. The second stretch focuses on the longest of the quads, which starts above the hip joint. This one improves your gait; if you're a sprinter, your time will improve. Because the longest quad is attached above the hip, this stretch can also help relieve lower-back and hip pain. It's really good for runners, soccer and baseball players, and dancers.

For the general stretch, you need a support about a foot high, or at a height that allows you to comfortably rest the front of your foot (instep) on it.

1. General Quad Stretch

Kneel on the floor with the support behind you. Bring your left foot forward and place it flat on the floor, with the left knee bent 90 degrees. Prop your right foot on the support. Your left hand is on your left thigh, with the elbow hanging off the side of the thigh. Your right hand is on your right hip. Chin-tuck your head.

> **Important:** if you have any kind of knee problem, place a cushion or other padding under your right knee. Make sure you have no knee discomfort. If you need two pillows to be completely comfortable, use them.
>
> I also like to put a rolled towel under my instep, so my right foot can bend normally.

Move your hips backward, so your buttocks come as close to your right heel as possible. Clench your buttocks, and keeping them clenched, bend at the hip joint, tighten your abdominal muscles, and lean your torso forward about 30 degrees. Press the top of your right foot down on the support.

> Some people can touch the buttocks to the heel; others won't. Either way is fine.

Keeping your torso bent forward and your buttocks and abs tensed, push your hips forward, keeping the right foot pressed down against the support. Hold for twenty seconds, rest for ten seconds, and then hold for another thirty seconds (see Figure 7-16).

Repeat this stretch on the left side.

FIGURE 7-16

TAPE LOOP

> Is my right foot pressing down firmly on the support?
> Is my head in the chin-tuck position?
> Am I leaning forward slightly?
> Are my abs tensed and my buttocks firmly clenched?
> Imagine the muscles as a broad band being pulled along the top of your thigh.

WHAT IT SHOULD FEEL LIKE

This is a pleasant, gratifying stretch. The muscles feel like a broad band about 3 inches wide being released from the hip to the knee.

2. Long Quad Stretch

Sit on your heels, and then lean back, supporting yourself on your hands behind you. Chin-tuck your head, lift your chest, and clench your buttocks. Press your hips up, imagining them moving at a 45-degree angle toward the wall in front of you. Hold for twenty seconds, rest for ten seconds, and then hold for another thirty seconds (see Figure 7-17).

You can have your palms flat on the floor or keep the palms off the floor and support yourself on your fingers. Try moving your hands wider apart or pointing the fingers out to the sides. Experiment to find the

FIGURE 7-17

hand position that feels most stable. Your goal is to lean back as far as you can. Ideally, your buttocks are almost touching your heels and your body is straight from the shoulders to the knees.

If you're more flexible, when you press upward your hips will move more vertically, toward the ceiling. If you're less flexible, they'll move more in a forward direction, toward the wall.

Caution: if you have extremely tight knees that can't bend deeply, do just the general stretch for a week, and see whether it releases your thigh muscles enough to enable you to do this one. If you still can't, put a couple of pillows under your buttocks so your knees don't have to bend as much. Be very careful with this stretch: if you push tight knees too hard, you can injure yourself.

TAPE LOOP

> Is my head in the chin-tuck position?
> Is my chest raised?
> Are my hips pushing upward?
> Am I leaning back as far as I can?
> Imagine the muscle as a wide band being pulled from above your hip to your knee.

WHAT IT SHOULD FEEL LIKE

You feel this stretch along the tops of your thighs from the groin to the knees. It's similar to the general stretch, but it's wider and you feel it above the hip joint.

Buttocks Muscle Stretch

The buttocks, or gluteus, muscles are primary core muscles, and you want them to be strong. Unfortunately, if you spend hours each day sitting, your glutes get zapped in two ways. First, they're compressed by the weight bearing into them. Second, they must remain stretched out to allow you to be in a sitting posture. Although these muscles must be stretched to break up scar tissue, they should not remain in a weak, overstretched condition. The strengthening program in Chapter 8 will strengthen the entire back of the body, including the buttocks muscles. But if you have the time, it's a good idea to do the Hip Flexor Stretch, which strengthens the glutes, in addition to the Buttocks Muscle Stretch until you're ready to start strengthening.

The Buttocks Muscle Stretch helps you walk better, since tight buttocks muscles slow the gait and also make you vulnerable to lower-back pain. Weak glutes also make it harder to lift heavy objects such as groceries or a child.

Sit on the edge of a chair and cross your right leg over the left. Bend *both* feet so the toes point toward your shins. Then tilt both feet so their *outer* edges move toward the ankles and their *inner* edges move away from the ankles. (This is called everting the feet; see Figure 6-5 on page 90.)

> *Once you have bent and tilted your feet, only the heel of your left foot is on the floor.*

Wrap your arms around your bent right leg, and try to catch hold of your elbows with your hands.

> *As a student of jujitsu I learned that the human body offers many great handles to grab onto. The knob of the elbow is one of them, and this stretch takes advantage of it. But if you can't reach your elbows with your hands, that's OK—just hold onto your forearms as far up as you can reach.*

Chin-tuck your head, and raise your chest very strongly. Pull your shoulder blades forcefully together. Pull your right leg toward your chest with your arms. When you reach the point where you can't pull the leg any closer to you, contract your right inner thigh muscles, and try to use these muscles to bring the leg in a little closer. Hold for twenty seconds, rest for ten seconds, and then hold for another thirty seconds (see Figure 7-18).

The buttocks muscles are large and thick, so you need to exert a lot of strength—both pulling with your arms and contracting your inner thigh muscles—to get a good stretch in them.

As the flexibility of your buttocks muscles improves, increase the stretch by putting a book or other support at least 3 inches high under the foot that's on the floor.

Repeat on the left side.

FIGURE 7-18

TAPE LOOP

> Is my chest strongly raised?
> Is my head in the chin-tuck position?
> Are my inner thigh muscles contracting?
> Are my shoulder blades pulled backward?
> Are both feet bent and tilted?
> Imagine a broad piece of heavy stretch fabric being pulled out along the side of your buttock.

WHAT IT SHOULD FEEL LIKE

This is a gratifying, very pleasant stretch. You feel it in a broad, thick sheet of muscle on the side of the buttock.

Human Pinwheel

Named for the way your legs spread out on the floor, the Human Pinwheel is another of my favorite stretches. It affects a key muscle deep inside the pelvis, the obturator internus, that rotates the hip outward. Although this is a crucial muscle needed for many ordinary movements—including plain old walking—hardly anyone ever stretches it. If it's tight, it keeps the entire leg in an outwardly rotated position, which can lead to a variety of problems.

A tight hip rotator makes you toe out when you walk, leading eventually to hip, lower-back, foot, and knee problems. Also, holding the leg continually in this outwardly rotated position puts a muscular clamp on the sciatic nerve, which over time leads to sciatica.

Since the Human Pinwheel puts stress on the knees, it's particularly important to do it on a soft, padded surface.

Sit on the floor, leaning on your hands behind your back. Place your feet flat on the floor about 20 inches apart and bend your knees up. Flop both knees to the left and spread your legs out, keeping the knees bent in the pinwheel position. Move your right thigh so it's at a 45-degree angle from your torso. Your right foot is to the side and behind you. Your right knee is bent 90 degrees (see Figure 7-19).

To get the right thigh in the correct position, imagine a line running through your navel, at the exact middle of your body. The right thigh should extend out at a 45-degree angle from this line.

FIGURE 7-19
› Getting into position

Important: *if your right knee feels uncomfortable in any way, bend it at an angle less than 90 degrees at which you feel no discomfort.*

Walk your left foot to the *left* as far as you comfortably can, digging the heel and side of the left foot into the floor in front of you. The left knee is bent 90 degrees or

Cautions for the Human Pinwheel

> Bending a knee 90 degrees can stress the meniscus, which is the cartilage that cushions the joint. So begin by bending the right knee less than 90 degrees. Only if this doesn't hurt should you progress to the full 90 degrees. If you have any feeling of instability at the inside of the knee or if it hurts, *don't do this stretch*. In fact, never force yourself into any position.

> If you have been diagnosed with avascular necrosis of the hip, don't do this stretch initially. You must first get hands-on deep tissue work in and around the hip joint. Then you may be able to do the stretch under the supervision of your practitioner. Even so, progress slowly and systematically. Start with the easy version on a chair; then sit on a thick book or other support that raises you 2 to 3 inches off the floor. Only when your hip is stretched out should you get down on the floor itself.

less; it doesn't touch the floor. The right knee is on the floor, if possible. Bend both feet strongly back to bring the toes toward the shins.

The function of the left leg is to create traction that helps you stay in position.

Now hold your right arm in front of you, with the elbow straight and the inside of the elbow facing up. Your left hand is still supporting you on the floor. Bend your right wrist so the palm faces away from you, with your fingertips pointing toward the floor. Use your left hand to slowly push your body into a more erect position. When you feel you can balance without falling backward, bring the left arm and hand in front of you and put it in the same position as the right arm and hand.

People with tight forearm muscles won't be able to bend their wrists enough for the fingers to point downward. That's OK—just keep the full position in mind as your goal. You can also do the Inside-of-Forearm Stretch, which will help you bend your wrists farther.

Chin-tuck your head. Hold both arms out in front of you, as close to parallel as you can get them, and lift your chest. Keeping the chest lifted, slowly rotate your torso and arms to the right. Don't just move your arms—

make sure your torso itself twists. Push the arms away from you, keeping the elbows straight and chest lifted (see Figure 7-20).

If you're tight, your right sit bone (the sit bones are the bones you sit on at the bottom of your pelvis) will come off the floor. Don't worry—in time that sit bone will drop, as your rotator muscle becomes more flexible. As you twist, imagine the sit bone moving toward the floor.

EASY VERSION: *This is a tough stretch! One way to make it easier is to do the Inner Thigh stretches (page 150) before doing this one. Here are some other ways to make it easier:*

FIGURE 7-20
〉 Final position

> *If you are tight and can't spread your legs enough to sit upright, if you have knee pain, or if your right sit bone stays high up off the floor, use a telephone book or some kind of padding to lift your buttocks 2 to 3 inches.*

> *If using this support is still too difficult, sit on a chair that has no arms, spreading your legs out in the same way, but with your feet on the floor. From the chair, you can progress to a support on the floor and then eventually get down on the floor itself.*

> *There are also several options for working on the floor. If you can't balance without your hands supporting you behind your back, sit for a while in that position, letting gravity pull your right knee to the ground. Try pulsing the knee toward the floor a few times, and then wait and let it settle as close to the floor as it can get (but only do this if it feels OK). Then use your hands on the floor to walk your torso into the twist.*

Press the inner part of your right knee toward the floor. You'll notice that when you press the knee down, the sit bone pops up. Therein lies the challenge! Try to push the sit bone down *at the same time* that you press the knee down.

The Sit Bone Samba

Coax your sit bone toward the floor with a slow, sensual grinding movement. I call it the Sit Bone Samba. It's the same as the Sacral Samba I suggest for the Low Back Stretch (see page 108); only this time it's your sit bone that's moving toward the floor. The Sit Bone Samba makes a huge difference, particularly in the thirty-second hold.

Moving the sit bone toward the floor is the crux of the stretch, and it's very hard to do. Here's where the adjustment comes in: you need to juggle pressing the knee and then the sit bone, knee, sit bone, and so on, back and forth. Use a slow, gentle, but firm downward pressure. After a few sessions, you'll feel the stretch lock in as the muscle begins to let go. Even if the sit bone never actually reaches the floor, your intention is to keep progressing in that direction. This may take a while, but if you persevere you'll see big changes.

Hold for twenty seconds, and then put your hands behind you, catch your breath, and let your muscles relax for ten seconds. Now go back into the stretch for another thirty seconds. The rest period should give you extra gas to push a bit farther. Your intention is to increase the stretch by about 5 percent.

To come out of the stretch safely, lift your right knee slightly and walk your right toes to the left until the leg is in a comfortable position. Then use your right hand to scoop your thigh off the floor and gently move your leg out of position.

The Human Pinwheel is a precarious position that puts stress on your hip and knee. After the first twenty seconds or after the thirty-second hold, your hip may feel creaky or weak. Do not explode out of this position. Move very slowly so you don't feel any discomfort.

Repeat the stretch on the left side.

TAPE LOOP

> Is my head in the chin-tuck position?
> Is my chest lifted?
> Am I pushing my arms out from my shoulders with my elbows straight?
> Most important: Is my right sit bone moving toward the floor?
> Am I pressing my right knee into the floor?
> Am I keeping both feet bent upward toward my shin? (Most people forget this one.)
> Imagine the right sit bone slowly dropping closer to the floor.
> Imagine your right thigh as a log rolling inward.

WHAT IT SHOULD FEEL LIKE

During the twenty-second hold, you feel a tightness in your groin and in the outside of your hip that may be slightly uncomfortable. In the thirty-second hold, this discomfort diminishes or disappears completely. But you feel a very deep stretch in the side of your hip. When you come out of position, you may feel creaky. This is normal. You're stretching a muscle you probably never stretched before, so you can expect it to feel strange.

Inner Thigh Spectrum

This series (or, as I like to say, spectrum) of three stretches targets three of the inner thigh muscles, called adductors, whose job is to move the legs toward each other. Hardly anyone recognizes the importance of these muscles, which become pretty tight in anyone who spends much time sitting. The Inner Thigh Spectrum is good for lower-back problems, because two of the muscles attach to the pubic bone. If they're tight, they exert a strong downward and outward force that creates pain by distorting the normal movement of the lower back.

Dancers, who raise their legs above their heads and shoot their legs out to the side, and skaters, who use these muscles to push off, both develop considerable scarring in the inner thigh and really need these stretches.

The first stretch affects all three muscles. The second one targets the shortest of the muscles, which goes from the groin to the top of the thighbone. This one is particularly good for inline skaters. The third stretch affects the longest of the muscles, which starts at the groin and runs to a point a few inches above the knee.

For best results, use a support about 6 to 8 inches high and wide enough to rest your elbows on. One or two couch cushions or some phone books will do. If you can't come up with any kind of support, you can do these stretches with your elbows on the floor, but they work better if your upper-body weight bears down from a raised position.

Since there are three stretches in the Inner Thigh Spectrum, I've adjusted the timing to keep them simple. All three use the same tape loop (page 154).

1. General Inner Thigh Stretch

Kneel on the floor, and lean your forearms on your support. Your elbows are shoulder width apart, and you're standing on your knees with your calves, thighs, and hips all at 90-degree angles. Walk your knees out to the sides, one step at a time, alternating knees until they're almost as far apart as you can get them—leave a bit of slack for stretching. The knees should still be bent at 90-degree angles. Chin-tuck your head.

Point your toes out to each side, and strongly bend both feet so the toes point back toward the shins. Press the insides of your heels into the floor. As you do this, your hips start to sink downward.

Keep your back straight and your head in the chin-tuck position as your groin starts to stretch. Slowly and carefully, walk your knees out a bit more—½ inch at a time—until you're close to your maximum amount of stretch.

Now press your hips toward the floor by contracting your buttocks. As you press down, your knees slide a bit farther apart. This is great—it's what you're aiming for! Once you are fully in position, hold for ten seconds (see Figure 7-21).

FIGURE 7-21

There's a tendency to arch the back as you press your hips downward. Be careful not to do this!

There's also a tendency to relax the feet from their bent position and let the heels come up off the floor. Check these points as part of your tape loop, and do your best to stay in position.

To come out of the stretch, begin by walking your knees back to center, ½ inch with each step. *Do not* arch your back as you do this. Rest a few seconds, and then move directly to the Upper Inner Thigh Stretch.

If you are not careful getting out of the stretch, you risk tearing the inner thigh muscles.

WHAT IT SHOULD FEEL LIKE

You feel a cordlike pull in your groin. This can be uncomfortable, so be gentle with yourself and stretch only to that point of slight discomfort I've described.

2. Upper Inner Thigh Stretch

Lean your arms on your support, and position the rest of your body as in the General Inner Thigh Stretch. But this time, swing your heels out so your knees are bent at an angle wider than 90 degrees. This means your feet are farther apart than your knees.

FIGURE 7-22

Move your elbows about 2 inches forward on your support, or until you feel a stretch in the upper part of your inner thighs. You may need to move your elbows as much as 6 inches forward; as you do this, your torso comes down closer to the support. Clench your buttocks, and press your hips down toward the floor. Hold for ten seconds (see Figure 7-22).

You may need to move the support itself some distance forward.

To come out of the stretch, walk your forearms backward, walk your knees bit by bit back to center, and sit back on your heels. Rest a few seconds, and then move directly to the Lower Inner Thigh Stretch.

WHAT IT SHOULD FEEL LIKE

You feel a stretch similar to that in the General Inner Thigh Stretch, except that it's focused on the upper part of your thigh, close to the groin.

3. Lower Inner Thigh Stretch

Take the same position as for the previous two inner thigh stretches, except that now you bring your heels as close together as possible. Walk your elbows backward on your support (moving the support itself if you need to), and then contract your buttocks and press your hips down toward the floor. Make sure you're also pressing your heels into the floor. Hold for ten seconds (see Figure 7-23).

FIGURE 7-23

Come out of the stretch by walking your forearms forward and then walking your knees together.

WHAT IT SHOULD FEEL LIKE

This version, with the heels close together, affects the lower inner thigh muscle, so you should feel a stretch in that area. You may also feel it in the mid inner thigh.

After a ten-second rest, decide which of the three inner thigh muscles was the tightest—that is, which stretch was hardest to do. Do only that stretch for thirty seconds, sliding your knees ½ inch farther out on each side; this enables you to put in the extra 5 percent effort. If all three muscles were tight, pick one that you feel like doing. Stretch this one for several sessions, until it feels a lot looser than the others. Then pick another muscle, and stretch it the same way. Your goal is to work these muscles until they're all equally stretched out.

Here you're truly your own therapist, diagnosing and fixing your own problem. Once you've released all three inner thigh muscles, you can test them periodically by doing the three stretches. If one or two muscles have tightened up (usually those that were tight originally), use the appropriate stretch to release them.

If you find that the muscles of one leg are significantly tighter than those of the other, use a mental device that I find is very helpful. Simply pay focused attention to the tight side. It automatically presses down harder, which balances out the two sides.

TAPE LOOP FOR INNER THIGH SPECTRUM

> Is my back flat, not arched?
> Are my feet still strongly bent?
> Are my heels touching the floor?
> Am I clenching my buttocks to push my pelvis toward the floor?
> Imagine your knees sliding smoothly apart, like a drop of ink spreading over a paper towel.

General Note for Inner Thigh Spectrum

You need to play around with this set of stretches to find the right adjustments for your own body. If you don't feel the effects I describe, try adjusting how far you spread your legs, how much you bend your knees, and how far forward or backward you move your forearms and torso.

Remember that during the thirty-second hold, you're looking to stretch 5 percent farther—a subtle but very significant increase. Here's a chance to practice listening to your body. During this hold, try spreading your legs a little more, and see what your body's response is. You'll find that this changes by the second: as the muscle opens up, what a moment ago felt like being stretched as far as you could go suddenly gives a little bit more.

Once you achieve the 5 percent, you can ask for that extra 1 percent. Use a very gentle pubic samba. With my buttocks contracted, I shift side to side in small circles, in very slow, measured movements. (Also see the samba instructions on pages 108 and 148.) The samba is a powerful tool, a subtle way of activating Sherrington's law without pushing yourself too hard.

Long Inner Thigh Stretch

While the Inner Thigh Spectrum targets three short inner thigh muscles (adductors), there's also a longer muscle that runs down the inner thigh from the pubic bone to the lower part of the inside of the knee. This stretch affects that muscle, the gracilis, which is essential for knee stability. If it's tight, it causes knee problems, especially when the medial meniscus, a crescent-shaped cartilage that cushions the inner knee, wears down, causing knee pain with clicking and popping inside the knee.

You need a low table, or a chair or stool that is not on wheels. Put a towel or soft pad on the top. You can also use a bed, as long as it's not too soft, or the armrest of a sofa. The support you choose depends on how high you can raise your leg. If you're really tight, try using a low step of a staircase. If you're very flexible, your support could be at waist level. Most people do fine with the support around knee level. Pick a support that doesn't make you stretch to your maximum. You should feel a moderate amount of slack in the inner thigh, because you'll be tightening it further.

Put your right heel up on the support. Slide your leg all the way out to the right, as far as it can comfortably go. Rotate your entire right leg to the right and bend the foot so the toes point back toward you. Rest your left hand on your left hip.

Place your right hand on your right thigh just above the kneecap, and apply gentle pressure diagonally downward, to the left. Lift your chest, and chin-tuck your head. Rotate your torso to the left as far as it can go.

Clench your right buttock, and imagine your right sit bone moving diagonally *behind* you to the right. Now firmly contract the muscles on the front of your right thigh (quadriceps). Hold twenty seconds, rest for ten seconds, and then hold again for thirty seconds (see Figure 7-24).

The backward movement of the sit bone is subtle and tricky, since clenching the buttocks naturally tends to move the pelvis forward. But it's the key to stretching this muscle. Experiment with how far you rotate your torso to the left, the angle of the pressure on your thigh, and the angle of backward movement of the right buttock, until you can feel the muscle stretching. If you feel it at the inside of the knee, you know you have the right one.

Caution: *the gracilis is a very thin muscle, and you can tear it if you stretch too aggressively. So respect this muscle, and work it carefully.*

Repeat on the left side.

FIGURE 7-24

TAPE LOOP

> Is my chest lifted?
> Is my head in the chin-tuck position?
> Is my foot bent?
> Is my knee straight?
> Is my leg rotated to the right?
> Is my torso rotated to the left?
> Am I pressing my right buttock diagonally backward?
> Imagine a long, thin band being stretched from the lower inside part of your knee up to the pubic bone.

WHAT IT SHOULD FEEL LIKE

The muscle should feel like a long, thin band being pulled from your groin to the inside of your knee, along the bottom of the inside of your thigh.

Hamstring Spectrum

The Hamstring Spectrum is a series of three stretches targeting the three muscles that run down the back of the thigh. Tight hamstrings restrict running speed, jumping, and even walking. They force you to walk slower than normal—and slow walking wastes energy. The optimal walking speed for using your energy most efficiently is 3.4 miles per hour, and releasing the hamstrings with these three stretches enables you to walk at least this fast. If you're a runner, your speed will increase. The Hamstring Spectrum is also good for lower-back pain, knee pain, Achilles tendonitis, plantar fasciitis, Morton's neuroma (painful swelling of a nerve in the foot), and chronic ankle sprains.

You need a low table, or a chair or stool that is not on wheels. Put a towel or soft pad on the top. You can also use a bed, as long as it's not too soft, or the armrest of a sofa. The support you choose depends on how high you can raise your leg. If you're really tight, try using a low step of a staircase. If you're very flexible, your support could be at waist level. Most people do fine with a support around knee level. Pick a support that doesn't make you stretch to your maximum. Your hamstrings should have a moderate amount of slack, because you'll be tightening them further.

Since there are three hamstring stretches, I've adjusted the timing to keep them simple. All three use the same tape loop (page 160).

1. Middle Hamstring Stretch

Put your right heel on your support, and bend the toes back toward you. Then tilt your foot so the outer edge moves *away* from you and the inner edge comes *toward* you. This movement is called inverting the foot; see Figure 6-11 on page 101.

Interlace your fingers and place your interlocked hands *just above* your kneecap, *not* on it. Press your palms into your thigh.

Make sure your hands are no more than 1 inch or so above the upper edge of the kneecap. This position gives you the most leverage.

Raise your chest to flatten your back, and pull your shoulder blades toward each other. Then chin-tuck your head.

Keeping your back flat and chin tucked, begin to lean your torso forward. Lean just to the point where you feel a stretch behind your calf, knee, and thigh.

FIGURE 7-25

Expect to feel tension behind your calf, directly behind your knee, and in the lower part of the back of your thigh. You may even feel it all the way to the buttock.

Now tense the muscles of the *top* of the right thigh, while applying moderate pressure down into the thigh with your hands.

Tensing the quadriceps is essential to activate Sherrington's law: this action releases the hamstrings at the back of the thigh. You must feel those quadriceps tense vigorously under your palms. Most runners I've observed don't stretch their hamstrings properly. They therefore never address the fascia of these muscles, which is what you're stretching here.

Lean forward a bit more, aiming the middle of your chest toward your toes. Arch your back, and keep your shoulder blades pulled backward (see Figure 7-25). Hold for ten seconds, rest a few seconds, and then move directly to the Outer Hamstring Stretch.

Make a major effort to lift your chest—more than you think you need to—and push your shoulder blades together. Remember not to lose the straightness of your back and the tilt of your foot. All these actions are crucial to lock the fascia into place and focus the stretch on your hamstrings.

WHAT IT SHOULD FEEL LIKE

The Hamstring Spectrum is very different from standard hamstring stretching, and the stretches should be uncomfortable. To me, each of these stretches feels as though someone has shined a flashlight into my eyeballs—what I call a bright stretch. It really wakes me up. You feel it not just behind your thigh but also in your calf and even the soles of your feet, since all those muscles are part of the same fascial chain.

You feel the Middle Hamstring Stretch right down the middle of the back of your thigh.

2. Outer Hamstring Stretch

Keeping your right leg up on the support, move your hands ½ inch toward the *outside* of your thigh. Rotate your torso about 30 degrees toward that side. Then rotate your leg to the *inside*.

> *If you're flexible, you may need to rotate your torso more than 30 degrees to get the stretch—but no more than about 80 percent of your maximum. Save a little for the stretch. The basis of this action is that your thigh turns inward while your torso turns outward.*

Maintain both rotations as you go back into the same position as for the Middle Hamstring Stretch: foot bent and tilted, chest lifted, back straight, and chin tucked. Firmly tense your quadriceps, and press into them with your palms, using moderate pressure (see Figure 7-26). Hold for ten seconds. Rest a few seconds, and then move into the Inner Hamstring Stretch.

WHAT IT SHOULD FEEL LIKE

You feel the Outer Hamstring Stretch along the outside of the back of the thigh.

FIGURE 7-26

3. Inner Hamstring Stretch

Keep your leg on the support, but this time, move your hands ½ inch from center toward the *inside* of your thigh. Rotate your torso about 30 degrees inward, and your thigh slightly outward. Maintain these rotations while you go back into position: foot bent and tilted, chest lifted, back straight, and chin tucked. Then tense the quadriceps firmly, and press into them with your hands. Hold for ten seconds, and then rest for ten seconds (see Figure 7-27).

> *You may need to rotate your torso more than 30 degrees to get the stretch.*

FIGURE 7-27

WHAT IT SHOULD FEEL LIKE

You feel the Inner Hamstring Stretch along the inside of the back of the thigh.

After the ten-second rest, decide which of the three hamstring muscles was the tightest—that is, which stretch was hardest to do. Do just this one for thirty seconds, putting in the extra 5 percent effort. If all three muscles were tight, pick one that you feel like doing. Stretch this one for several sessions, until it feels a lot looser than the others. Then pick another hamstring and stretch it the same way. Your goal is to work these muscles until they're all equally stretched out.

Here again you're truly your own therapist, diagnosing and fixing your own problem. Once you've released them all, you can test them periodically by doing all three stretches. If one or two muscles have tightened up (usually the ones that were tight originally), you can use the appropriate stretch to release them.

Last, repeat the entire sequence with the left leg.

TAPE LOOP FOR HAMSTRING SPECTRUM

> Is my foot bent and tilted?
> Is my head in the chin-tuck position?
> Am I keeping my chest lifted and my shoulder blades pushed together?
> Is my back straight?
> Am I maintaining the correct opposing rotations of my torso and leg in the Outer Hamstring and Inner Hamstring stretches?
> Are my hands close to the upper edge of my kneecap, not 2 to 3 inches above it?
> Am I firmly contracting my quadriceps?
> Am I pressing down with my palms?
> Imagine a long piece of taffy being stretched out in the back of your thigh, extending from your upper calf to your buttocks.

Calf Muscle Stretch

We clearly need the calf muscle (gastrocnemius) for walking and running. But when it's contracted, it contributes to body problems that aren't so obvious. Since the calf muscle is part of the fascial chain that runs from the bottom of the feet all the way up the back of the body, it affects the entire chain when it is tight. This means that a tight calf can be a cause of lower-back pain, knee pain, shin splints, chronic sprained ankles, Morton's neuroma (painful swelling of a nerve in the foot), arthritis of the toes, and bunions. The Calf Muscle Stretch helps improve all these conditions. What's more, if you have difficulty getting your legs up the wall for the Low Back Stretch, do this stretch first—it will help you with the other.

The Calf Muscle Stretch includes two movements, which stretch the two halves of the muscle. You need a wall plus a strap, belt, or towel long enough to loop over your foot when your leg is extended.

Find a spot where you can lie on your back with your legs up on the wall. You need enough room on either side to swing your legs around and up on the wall in a windshield-wiper movement.

Place a mat or blanket right up against and touching the wall. Sit on the mat with the left side of your body against the wall. Your hip and knee should touch it. Lean back on your elbows and raise your left leg, walking it up the wall. Then walk the right leg up the wall, swinging your torso around to face the wall. As you do this, keep your buttocks in contact with the wall, or as close to it as you can. Now lie down and flatten your back so it's completely in contact with the floor while your legs rest on the wall.

If your hamstrings, calves, and lower back are tight, you won't be able to keep your buttocks against the wall and also straighten your knees. Don't feel bad—most people find either that their butt is 3 to 4 inches off the wall or that their legs are bent. If you're uncomfortable, slide your buttocks away from the wall as much as you need to.

Straighten your right leg as much as you can against the wall. Even if you can't straighten your knee completely, make sure the leg is perfectly vertical. Bend your left knee slightly, and let the left leg rest against the wall. Your head rests on the floor.

FIGURE 7-28
> Foot everted

Either the sole or the side of the left foot can rest against the wall—whichever is more comfortable.

Work your buttocks as close to the wall as you can get them, and straighten your right knee as much as you can. Loop the towel or strap over the arch of your right foot, and hold the ends with both hands.

Firmly bend your foot so your toes come toward you. Then pull on the strap with your right hand to tilt your foot (like pulling on a horse's reins), so the outside edge comes closer to you and the inside edge moves away from you. (This is called everting the foot; see Figure 7-28.) Maintain the pull on the strap while you press your sacrum into the floor as firmly as possible. Do a brief Sacral Samba, slowly grinding one side and then the other side of your sacrum into the floor, twice on each side (see page 108). Hold twenty seconds, rest for ten seconds, and then hold for another thirty seconds.

Don't pull hard on the towel; use it very gently. Ninety percent of the work to bend the foot should come from the shin muscle that runs along the front of the leg bone. This muscle's action is essential to activate Sherrington's law and provide the therapeutic effect. The towel is essentially a fine-tuner.

The Sacral Samba is a slow, focused, internal movement, like a sensuous dance.

As your calf muscle becomes more flexible, work to straighten your knee until you can bring your heel away from the wall.

Now pull the strap with your left hand to tilt the foot in the opposite direction, so the outside edge tilts away and the inside edge comes closer (this is called inverting the foot; see Figure 7-29). Press your sacrum into the floor again, and do the Sacral Samba. Hold for twenty seconds, rest for ten seconds, and then hold for another thirty seconds.

Often people feel a stretch in the back of the thigh. This is normal. These muscles are part of the same chain, and all of it needs to be stretched.

Repeat the entire routine with the left leg.

FIGURE 7-29
› Foot inverted

TAPE LOOP

› Is my knee as straight as I can get it?
› Is my sacrum pressing firmly into the floor?
› Is my foot actively bending and tilting?

WHAT IT SHOULD FEEL LIKE

This is one of the bright stretches that really wakes you up. You should feel a strong pull from the sole of your foot all the way to the buttocks. Or you may feel it most in the upper half of the calf muscle and behind the knee.

Shin Muscle Stretch

This stretch releases a muscle that runs along the front of your shin and helps you bend your foot so you can walk properly. Tightness in this muscle (tibialis anterior) predisposes a person to ankle and foot problems such as Achilles tendonitis and heel pain. This muscle must be treated along with the muscles on the back of the leg to fix any problem involving the calf, foot, or ankle. The Shin Muscle Stretch improves your gait and reduces foot or ankle pain. Anyone with arthritic ankles really needs this stretch.

Sit on your heels, with the tops of your feet flat on the floor. Keep your left hand on the floor for balance. Hook the thumb of your right hand over the back of your right ankle (i.e., over the Achilles tendon) and press down with moderate force.

Lift your right knee until you feel a slight discomfort. Then strongly curl the toes of your right foot up toward the sole, trying to lift the entire front of the foot off the floor. Hold for twenty seconds and rest for ten seconds. Then during the thirty-second hold, lift the right knee as high as you can (see Figure 7-30).

You can hook the webbing between the thumb and palm around the Achilles tendon, instead of the thumb itself. Or try turning your hand around, so the palm faces backward.

Lifting the foot is important. That won't actually happen, but having the intent and trying to do it triggers Sherrington's law and releases the shin muscle.

Adjust how high you lift the knee and the degree of curling the toes according to your flexibility and comfort level. If you're very flexible, you can lean backward to put more pressure down into the Achilles tendon.

Caution: *if you find it difficult to bend your knees enough to sit directly on your heels, slide a pillow into the crease of the knees and sit on it. If it's not thick enough, fold it in half or use two pillows.*

Repeat on the left side.

FIGURE 7-30

TAPE LOOP

> Am I pressing down on my Achilles tendon with a moderate amount of pressure?
> Am I lifting my knee to a point of slight discomfort?
> Am I curling my toes up strongly?

WHAT IT SHOULD FEEL LIKE

The shin muscle feels like a thin strap being pulled. Most people feel the stretch at their instep and at the front of the ankle, and to some extent along the upper shin.

Sole-of-Foot Stretch

The major foot-moving muscles begin in the calf, but little muscles within the feet themselves help provide stability during movement. This stretch affects those little muscles. It makes the soles of your feet and your toes more flexible and improves gait and balance. If the soles are contracted and full of scar tissue, the GPS computers in these foot muscles don't work properly, and the feet can't make the necessary adjustments to keep your balance.

This stretch is great for preventing Achilles tendonitis and ankle sprains. It helps improve heel pain, plantar fasciitis, Morton's neuroma (painful swelling of a nerve), and arthritic toes. Dancers in particular need this stretch; so do runners and basketball and soccer players.

Many people have a great deal of scar tissue in the soles of their feet, which can make this stretch difficult. Doing the self-release technique for the sole of the foot (page 228) first may make this stretch much easier.

Caution: if you have acute, inflamed arthritis in your feet, don't do this stretch until the inflammation has gone down.

Sit on your heels. Lean forward a bit, lift your right foot, and prop it up on the toes. Use your hands at your sides on the floor to take some of your weight.

Sit back on your heels lightly—as much as you can tolerate. Tilt your right heel outward as far as necessary to put equal pressure on all five toes (see Figure 7-31). As the foot muscles release, you can lean backward to increase the pressure. Hold for twenty seconds, rest for five seconds, and then hold for another thirty seconds.

Repeat on the left side.

If you're really flexible, you can stretch both feet at once. Just be sure both feet are tilted outward so you are affecting all five toes equally.

Caution: *stretch very carefully. These tiny muscles are often severely scarred. If you push too hard, you can tear the fascia on the soles of the feet (plantar fascia).*

FIGURE 7-31

TAPE LOOP

〉 Do I feel equal pressure on all five toes?

WHAT IT SHOULD FEEL LIKE

This is an extremely intense stretch. You feel it all the way from the tips of the toes to the fronts of the heels.

CHAPTER EIGHT

Ming's Strengthening Program

Y ou've stretched, and you've seen a major change. Either your pain is completely gone, or it has decreased tremendously. But this improvement won't last unless you strengthen those stretched-out muscles and fascia. Strength is the engine that drives your ability to function day to day. Without it you will never achieve the well-being you seek.

Here's how to tell when you're ready to begin strength training:

> Your pain is below level 1 (barely noticeable).
> You can do the stretches almost perfectly.

Do not start this strengthening program when you're still in pain; your body has hot spots, bruises, and swellings; you have an acute injury; or you're sick: *you will hurt yourself.* Your body must be in proper condition before you can strengthen it safely and effectively.

169

I chose the strength-training exercises in this chapter carefully to make you injury-proof and posture perfect. My goal is not for you to look beautiful, although after a couple of months on this program, you will look beautiful. The program is simple, and there's just one program for everybody, no matter what their condition is. As I explained in Chapter 3, I don't believe in specific exercises for individual muscles. Instead, I've put together a series of routines that encompass in a very functional, natural way all the muscles that need strengthening. The program takes you to a level where your fascia and muscles are healthy and strong enough to prevent a recurrence of your pain and enable you to function well in everyday life. To increase your strength beyond this level, you would need heavier weights and more reps, but that's beyond the scope of this book.

Outline of the Program

In three twenty-minute workout sessions a week, you train each body part every fourth to fifth day. The program consists of two phases: building lean muscle and building strength and power. Strength is the amount of weight you can lift; power is how fast you can do it over time. Each phase includes two alternating sets of exercises, A and B. Set A works the upper body; set B works the lower body.

Phase 1: Building Lean Muscle

In the first few workout sessions, you just learn the movement patterns. Then you begin building lean, supple muscle. I like to say that lean tissue is the engine, not the payload. That is, you need lean tissue to get the result you're after: strength. The more muscle you have, the easier it is to build strength. Phase 1 is important especially for women, who tend to be chronically weak.

Phase 1 prepares you for strength-building at higher speeds in Phase 2. Most people need six to eight weeks for Phase 1 and possibly more if they choose to work through all the variations of the exercises. Frail or elderly people may need as long as twelve weeks to build enough lean muscle to move on to Phase 2. But even if they stay in Phase 1 and never make it to Phase 2, they can continue to train using the Kaizen principle of continuous small improvements. I guarantee they will still experience great improvement both in pain level and in daily functioning.

Phase 2: Building Explosive Strength

In Phase 2 you switch to explosive movements—sudden and fast—done at greater speed, with increasing reps and decreasing rest periods. Once you achieve the maximum number of reps given in the instructions (which should take about six weeks), you should be at an excellent level of strength, flexibility, and GPS functioning; the improvement in your everyday life will be dramatic. As a side benefit, you'll also achieve significant cardiovascular fitness. You'll be fine if you simply maintain this level of exercise for the rest of your life. But if you get inspired and decide to go further, you'll need to join a gym or buy heavier weights. Consult a qualified fitness trainer to find out what's right for you.

Cautions

People with the following conditions should be cautious and prudent when beginning a strength-training program:

> Strength training can increase blood pressure and strain the heart. If you have high blood pressure or a history of heart disease, consult a medical professional with sports or fitness expertise to find out whether this program is safe for you.

> Frail people should not exercise to the point where their pulse exceeds 110 beats per minute. Do 1 set of an exercise, and take your pulse. Use a pulse monitor, or count the number of beats for six seconds and multiply by 10 to get your total beats per minute. If your pulse is under 110, do another set and check again. Whenever your pulse goes above 110, rest longer than ninety seconds between sets—even as long as two minutes. Usually after a few workouts, you'll notice that exercising will not increase your heart rate as much. When you reach the point where your

Ming's Strengthening Program

Plan to do three workout sessions a week—Monday, Wednesday, and Friday—alternating sets A and B.

PHASE 1: BUILDING LEAN MUSCLE
Set A: Upper Body (above the hips)
> Dead Lift
> Curl and Press
> Progression Push-Ups (wall, knee, standard, raised-foot)

Set B: Lower Body (hips and below)
> Air Squat
> Split Squats (regular, with weights)
> Overhead Squat

PHASE 2: BUILDING EXPLOSIVE STRENGTH
Set A: Upper Body (above the hips)
> Two-Arm Swing
> Clean and Press
> Ballistic Push-Up

Set B: Lower Body (hips and below)
> Speed Squat
> Lunges (straight, 30-degree, with dumbbells)
> Overhead Squat with Additional Weight

pulse doesn't pass 110 for two weeks straight, it's time to slowly increase your reps and allow your pulse to go up to 120 and then 130. At that level you'll be quite fit and won't have to worry about your heart rate.

You Must Use Weights

This program depends on using weights. You need weights because building muscle and strength requires a significant amount of effort. Otherwise, you don't get results. My preferred all-around weight for strengthening the entire body beautifully is the kettlebell, but you can also use dumbbells or even weighted plastic jugs, although your results won't be as good. A couple of the exercises require holding a weight in each hand, which means either two dumbbells or two jugs. Ideally, you will have two kettlebells and two pairs of dumbbells of different weights.

If You Want to Stay Weak, Lift Light

The weights I recommend may seem quite heavy to you, especially if you're a small woman who has never lifted weights before. I've spent years in gyms and seen that many women use weights that are too light. Seeing women lifting 4-pound weights drives me crazy, because I know those weights won't do anything for them. It's a scientific fact that a light weight does not provide enough stimulation of the nervous system for muscle building or strength building to occur. Basically, it wastes your time. Go lift a heavy frying pan or carry a bag of groceries upstairs—you'll get a better workout. Believe me when I tell you that you will be able to handle weights considerably heavier than you imagine.

Not to let men off the hook—they, too, lift weights that are too light, because their doctors tell them not to strain. But you have to strain some. Making a real effort is the genesis of building muscle and strength. That's why I say, if you want to stay weak, keep lifting light.

The beautiful thing about the Ming program is that it's built on the Kaizen principle of continuous small improvements. This means that even very weak people can succeed in a progressive strengthening program by starting off with lighter weights. Your goal is to get tiny little changes in every workout, imperceptible to everyone except yourself. Thirty days later, you have a huge change. Sixty days later, the difference is like night and day.

Kettlebells

Several of my exercises use the kettlebell, an old-fashioned Russian weight that looks like a ball with a handle. I'm a big fan of the kettlebell. Its shape and its handle make it easier to swing than a dumbbell of equal weight. If you're used to lifting a dumbbell, you'll find that the kettlebell feels different because of its weight distribution.

Kettlebells come in a range of weights. Prices vary; you can find the best values online. Low price does *not* indicate poor quality. Look for a large handle, which makes the bell easier to swing with two hands. You must be able to get at least three fingers of both hands, plus the thumbs, through the handle. Two fingers is not enough—you won't be able to hold on to it when it swings.

If you go the kettlebell route, buy one of each suggested weight, according to the rough guidelines that follow. Start with the lighter one, and switch to the heavier one as you get stronger. The list includes different weights for people who don't exercise and are not athletic, and those who are. If possible, try them out in a store or practice in a gym with a professional trainer to learn more precisely which weights are right for you. Kettlebell weights are often given in kilograms (1 kg is 2.2 pounds).

> Women less than 140 pounds: 4 kilograms and 8 kilograms
> Women more than 140 pounds: 6 kilograms and 8 kilograms
> Athletic women of any size: 6 kilograms and 12 kilograms
> Men less than 180 pounds: 6 kilograms and 12 kilograms
> Men more than 180 pounds: 8 kilograms and 16 kilograms
> Athletic men of any size: 12 kilograms and 20 kilograms

These numbers may seem quite high. But believe me, even the frailest people can handle an 8-kilogram or 12-kilogram (18- or 26-pound) kettlebell. I've set these weights at levels anyone can manage, because the goal here is not to turn you into a bodybuilder but simply to keep you out of pain.

Dumbbells

If you choose to use dumbbells, make sure they're the *fixed-weight* type, not the adjustable kind that you load weights onto, since you'll be swinging them fast and you don't want anything that can fly off the end. You'll need two pairs, one pair of each weight.

> Women less than 140 pounds: 10 pounds and 15 pounds
> Women more than 140 pounds: 12 pounds and 15 pounds
> Athletic women of any size: 12 pounds and 15 pounds
> Men less than 180 pounds: 12 pounds and 15 pounds
> Men more than 180 pounds: 15 pounds and 25 pounds
> Athletic men of any size: 20 pounds and 25 pounds

Plastic Jugs

If you don't want to buy weights at all, you can use large plastic jugs with handles, such as liquid laundry detergent containers. Look for jugs with the largest handles you can find. A gallon of detergent weighs about 8 pounds, which is heavy enough to do one-arm swings and, for people who aren't very strong, two-arm swings. You can also fill a jug with sand, adding a precise amount to make the jug exactly the right weight. Make sure you fasten the cap well; you'll be swinging the jug fast, and if the cap flies off, you'll wind up with a cleaning disaster.

Since jugs can substitute for either dumbbells or kettlebells, adjust the weight depending on what you're using them for.

Some Strength-Training Basics

To get the most out of this program, you need to know a bit about how strength training works. It's actually quite scientific. The number of reps in a set, the progression of exercises, and especially the use of heavy-enough weights all affect how your body responds to exercise and determine whether you reach your goals.

The exercise instructions give different rep ranges for men and for women. This is because certain inescapable physiological differences affect men's and women's relative strengths, and therefore also the way they should train and the results they can achieve. First, men are generally larger than women. As a rule, the larger your body mass, the stronger you are. Second, men have more testosterone, which makes it easier for them to gain lean body mass and strength. Third, men generally have a larger proportion of fast-twitch muscle fibers, which means they can lift heavier weights than women of the same body weight. And last, I've observed that women tend to have less upper-body strength, even when both are equally trained.

Of course, there are exceptions. Some women are stronger than many men; some men are weaker than many women. If you're unsure, always start with the suggested lighter weight. If the workout feels too difficult, *don't* decrease the weight, but do 1 less rep per set. If the workout feels too easy, that's a sign to do 1 to 2 more reps per set. Don't move to a heavier weight for any exercise until you can do, in perfect form, the highest number of reps given in the instructions. "Perfect form" means that the last rep is *identical* to the first rep, except that as you fatigue, you slow down very slightly on the upstroke. Thus you may be doing some exercises with the heavier weight, while still doing others with the lighter weight.

Tempo

Your tempo is the speed and rhythm of your upstroke and downstroke as you lift a weight or your body in the push-ups and squats. Few trainers talk about tempo, but it's extremely important. A slow tempo (2 seconds up and 3 seconds down) puts your muscles under tension for a longer period, and the longer the tension, the more lean tissue you get. A faster tempo (0.5 second up and 1 second down) builds more fast-twitch fibers and thus more power and speed.

That's why it's important to follow the speed instructions I give in the exercises. Phases 1 and 2 have a couple of similar exercises, but since they are done at different tempos, they build different fibers.

Note that these speeds are *guidelines*. No one can get their tempo exact to 0.5 second. Just do the best you can, counting in your head, "One and two and . . ."

The Concept of Intent

Intent is a critical concept in strength training. It means applying great energy and determination to your workout, an intense mental focus and desire to get it just right. Tackling your workout with a strong intent tremendously magnifies its power. The input from your mind stimulates your nervous system, which is what tells the muscle fibers to contract. This means that the stronger your mental drive, the more muscle fibers you activate and the more vigorously they contract. Without intent, you won't progress very far. So psych yourself up before you start.

Part of intent is not getting distracted. Don't talk, don't let your mind wander, and keep your head in neutral position. Your goal is to be completely present in your body. Pretend you're driving a car at 160 miles per hour. It's actually *dangerous* to turn or tilt your head in the middle of a set, since this movement weakens the side that the head turns to and throws off the entire GPS system. Many people have full-blown conversations with their trainers right in the middle of a hard set—which to me is the ultimate in risk. Or they do what I call the Stepford Wives workout, staring vacuously into space and thinking about other things. As I say to the people I train, "If a firecracker goes off 20 feet away, you don't even turn your head—you finish your set."

Intentional Breathing

Breathing is another crucial component of strength training. If you breathe casually with your mouth wide open, it's actually impossible to develop strength and power. Proper breathing reflects a strong, focused intent, which is why I call it "intentional breathing." It involves a forced exhalation during the exertion parts of the exercise, in which you puff your cheeks and blow air out forcefully through the small hole of your pursed mouth.

Forced exhalation temporarily increases the air pressure in your abdomen, which actually helps you lift by making the body stable and rigid, protecting your spine. It's like having a blown-up balloon inside you that holds everything in place.

Breathe rhythmically, exhaling on the exertion part of every rep, never holding your breath, and never taking in too much air. At more than 10 reps per set, people sometimes breathe with their mouth open too wide. They take in and push out too much air and get dizzy. Inhale through your nose, taking in just enough air to do the rep. This may seem like a lot to remember, but after a couple of sessions intentional breathing becomes natural. You'll feel it as part of the lift and won't have to think about it again.

Intentional breathing also has a psychological effect: it focuses your mind on your intent and revs you up to lift more correctly and more aggressively, increasing the energy of your workout.

Resting

Adequate rest periods are critical to the success of strength training. I see too many people in gyms undermining their efforts to build strength by not resting long enough. By the last rep in a set, you'll be a bit fatigued. Your nervous system and the rest of your body need a certain amount of time to reboot and come back to a state close to normal. If you don't rest long enough after the first set, you won't perform as well in the second set, and the third set will be a mess.

Make sure you rest sitting down; this is the time to take deep breaths if you want to. For most exercises, the minimum rest period is sixty seconds, but most people need ninety seconds. Gauge the amount of time you need by the following indicators:

> ❯ Your breathing should be 90 percent of normal.
> ❯ The muscles that were working (e.g., lower back, quads, buttocks) should feel only a very small amount of fatigue.
> ❯ You should feel mentally alert.

If you're not sure, take the extra thirty seconds. Always err on the side of extra rest.

Dress for Warmth and Protection

As with stretching, you must make sure your body is warm when doing strength training. If the room is chilly, wear a long-sleeved T-shirt or sweatshirt and long exercise pants. I see many people training in highly air-conditioned gyms wearing tank tops and shorts. That's a huge mistake: first, because it's easy to pull a muscle that's cool, and second, because the

Young Again!

A sixty-one-year-old businessman asked me to train him. He had been working out in a gym, but his technique was shaky and imprecise. He also liked inline skating for long distances, but his lower back and legs fatigued easily, so he had to stop and rest often.

Instead of training him right away, I taught him some stretches. He did the Dead Roach 1, Low Back, and Hip Flexor stretches for three weeks to release his neck, lower-back, and hip fascia and to make his GPS system work more efficiently. Only then did he progress to building lean muscle. The stretches had a dramatic effect on his ability to do dead lifts and squats. Previously, he couldn't bend down easily, and he wobbled badly when doing squats. But two weeks post-stretching, he was like a metronome: up, down, in perfect rhythm and form.

In the middle of the muscle-building program, he noticed that he felt much stronger while skating. He found himself bounding up subway stairs much faster. And there was a big difference when he made love to his girlfriend, the result of stretching out his hip flexor muscles and strengthening his buttocks and lower back. He had far more endurance, and he felt much more powerful. As he put it: "Wow! I feel young again!"

joints are more lubricated, the fascia is more gelatinous, and the muscles contract more forcefully when warm, giving you a far better workout.

It's also a good idea to wear exercise sneakers, not only to get better traction, but also because they provide some protection if you drop a weight on your foot.

GENERAL WARM-UP

You must be warmed up to do strength training. Warming up lubricates your joints, revs up your nervous system, and increases your body temperature enough to induce a slight sweat, which is the key sign that you're ready to begin the workout. In addition to firing up the nerves in your muscles and joints, you need alertness in your brain. If you feel mentally dull and uninspired, your body won't be ready to work out, which puts you at risk for injury. That's why I cannot overstate the importance of *a thorough, proper warm-up.*

If you have a warm-up you like, use it as long as you move your body vigorously for two to three minutes, break a slight sweat, and feel mentally and physically alert. The following is my own suggested routine. Whatever warm-up you do, rest for sixty seconds afterward before you start training.

Calf Raises (10 RAISES = 15 SECONDS)

Standing with your hands on your hips, come up onto your toes (see Figure 8-1). If you have trouble balancing, hold on to a wall or table at first. But work toward balancing on your own as soon as possible. Balancing is part of the warm-up; it stimulates the firing of your nervous system.

FIGURE 8-1

Knee Circles (10 IN EACH DIRECTION = 40 SECONDS)

With your feet together, hold the sides of your thighs right above the knees with your hands. Make circles with your knees, 10 circles one way and 10 the other way (see Figure 8-2). If you have difficulty balancing, hold on to a table or chair with one hand.

FIGURE 8-2

Leg Swings (10 SWINGS EACH LEG = 30 SECONDS)

Standing, hold on to a chair with one hand, and swing one leg back and forth 10 times (see Figure 8-3). Then swing the other leg. (One swing includes both back and forth.)

FIGURE 8-3

Torso Circles (5 IN EACH DIRECTION = 20 SECONDS)

Stand with your hands on your hips and your feet slightly wider than shoulder width apart. Make circles with your torso, starting small and widening the circles as your flexibility increases (see Figure 8-4).

FIGURE 8-4

Toe Touches (5 REPS = 10 SECONDS)

Stand with your hands on your hips and your feet 6 to 8 inches apart. Bend down to touch your toes, or as far down as you can go. Bend your knees comfortably while doing this—even if you can touch your toes with your knees straight. Throughout, keep your eyes focused forward, not down, to stimulate your ability to balance (see Figure 8-5).

FIGURE 8-5

Toe Touch to Steeple (5 REPS = 15 SECONDS)

Stand with your feet 12 inches apart and your hands in front of you. Bend and touch your toes with bent knees. As you stand up, clasp your hands with the forefingers straight in steeple position. Stretch up as high as you can, so the steeple points toward the ceiling (see Figure 8-6). You should feel a nice stretch in your back and shoulders. Come down to starting position.

FIGURE 8-6

Alternating Arm Swings (10 REPS = 20 SECONDS)

Standing, simultaneously raise your right arm forward and your left arm backward. Swing them to reverse positions (see Figure 8-7). Do 10 swings (i.e., the right arm comes forward 10 times). Swing as high in each direction as you can without forcing the movement. Keep your knees bent and your torso leaning slightly forward.

FIGURE 8-7

Neck Circles (3 IN EACH DIRECTION = 10 SECONDS)

Standing, rotate your neck and head very gently, first in one direction and then in the other (see Figure 8-8). Move slowly, or you may get dizzy.

FIGURE 8-8

PHASE 1: BUILDING LEAN MUSCLE
SET A: UPPER BODY

Dead Lift

In the Dead Lift, the weight is raised from the floor to hip level. This exercise strengthens the lower back, quadriceps, and buttocks. It's good for preventing lower-back pain.

The Dead Lift uses one weight—a kettle-bell, dumbbell, or plastic jug. Start with your lighter weight.

Stand with your feet about 2 inches wider than hip width and turned out 30 degrees. Place the weight in front of you, halfway between your feet. During the entire exercise, hold your neck firmly and keep your head tilted up *slightly*, except briefly when you look down to grab the weight.

FIGURE 8-9

If your hips are tight and your balance poor, your stance can be slightly wider, with your feet turned out a little bit more. As you become more flexible, progressively narrow your stance and turn your feet out less.

Bend forward with a flat back, shoulders pulled back slightly, and head in neutral. Bend your knees, and grab the weight, keeping your back perfectly flat. Contract your abdominal muscles to protect your lower back. Grasp the weight firmly, and stand up, lifting the weight. Tuck your buttocks in as you come to standing position (see Figure 8-9).

When you stand, your torso should actually come 1 inch farther back than vertical, to ensure that the spinal muscles and buttocks fully contract.

FIGURE 8-10

Bend forward, keeping your back flat and abdominals slightly contracted, until the weight is about 2 inches above the floor (see Figure 8-10). Raise the weight again as before.

Some people can't bend down this far with a flat back. If you find yourself rounding your back, stop at the point just before you have to round it. At each workout, you'll be able to bend down a bit farther with your back flat.

If you're using a dumbbell, it's easiest to hold it vertically, cupping both hands around the bell at the top end.

The handle of a plastic jug is on the side, so the jug is more cumbersome to use because its weight is off center. However, you will get results as long as you use the right weight.

Inhale as you bend to pick up the weight; exhale as you lift it.

Do 3 sets of 8 reps, resting ninety seconds between sets. Each week, add 1 to 2 reps to each set. Your goal is 3 sets of 20 reps.

Once you reach that goal, start using your heavier weight and reset your reps to 6. If this is easy, go up 2 reps every workout; if it's not, go up just 1 rep. Build up again to 20 reps.

At this point, you can take it to the next level, if you like, by decreasing the rest period to sixty seconds. Doing that many reps with a shorter rest period is actually quite challenging, so don't worry if you never reach this goal—you're still doing yourself a lot of good.

Curl and Press

In a curl, the forearm lifts the weight from the thigh to the chest; in a press, the weight is lifted to the shoulder and then overhead. The Curl and Press works the biceps, triceps, rotator cuff, and shoulder and enhances coordination and balance. If you have a rounded back, the Curl and Press improves your posture. It's also quite a practical exercise, because it gives you that extra boost you need to put a heavy bag in an overhead compartment on a plane.

This exercise uses one weight—a kettlebell, dumbbell, or plastic jug. Start with your lighter weight.

This is a one-arm exercise. Stand in the same position as for the Dead Lift, but place the weight closer to your right foot. Your left arm is out to the side, acting as a counterbalance. Lean down, bending your knees with your back flat, and grab the weight with your right hand, palm facing away from you (see Figure 8-11). Come back to standing position (see Figure 8-12).

Keeping your elbow tucked against your ribs, lift your arm from the elbow, raising the weight to chin level. Turn your hand 45 degrees, so the palm faces diagonally out to the left (see Figure 8-13). Straighten

FIGURE 8-11

FIGURE 8-12

FIGURE 8-13

FIGURE 8-14

the arm and raise the weight forcefully overhead, decelerating its speed just before the elbow completely straightens out (see Figure 8-14).

The main mistake people make in this exercise is doing the press lackadaisically, without enough focus, intent, or energy. You need to push with vigor: straighten your arm with strong intent.

At the same time, make sure to decelerate just as the arm becomes straight, so you don't overextend your elbow and cause an injury. As you press, be mindful not to snap your elbow straight at the end point.

Bend your elbow to lower the weight to chin level. Turn your palm to face your shoulder and lower the forearm.

Exhale as you curl the weight to your shoulder and again as you press it up from your shoulder. Fit your inhalations in between the exhalations.

Do 1 set with the right arm; then put the weight down and rest for forty-five seconds. Then do 1 set with the left arm. After resting, do another set with the right arm. Continue alternating arms, and do 3 sets on each side.

Begin with 3 sets of 5 reps on each side. As you get stronger, add 1 rep per week. When 3 sets of 12 reps with a forty-five-second rest becomes too easy, start using your heavier weight and reset your reps to 5. Build up again to 3 sets of 12. Once you can handle this, decrease the rest period to thirty seconds.

To get to the next level, decrease the rest period to fifteen seconds.

Progression Push-Ups

Push-ups are a wonderful way to strengthen the upper body. In this program, you progress through four increasingly difficult push-up variations. Your goal is to complete a specified number of reps of one variation in perfect form before you move on to the next one. If you twist or hump your back or if your upward stroke visibly slows before *or on* the last rep, you must stop at this point for that workout.

This sounds rather authoritarian, but there are good reasons for it. First, if you don't perfect each variation before advancing to the next, you risk injury. Second, if your progressions aren't done honestly, you never know if you're truly getting stronger.

Following are general guidelines for all push-up variations:

> Your tempo should be 1.5 seconds up and 2 seconds down.
> Each time you progress to the next push-up variation, reset your reps down to 6 (5 is OK too, if 6 feels like too much). To progress, add 1 rep in each workout.

Wall Push-Up

Stand facing a wall and place your palms against it, about 1½ to 2 inches outside your shoulders on each side. Your fingers point toward the ceiling, with the fingertips at chin level. Step 2 to 3 feet away from the wall.

Your distance from the wall depends on your strength; the farther away you are, the more strength you need for the push-up. Two to three feet is right for the average person. If you are frail or weak, start out closer to the wall.

Push your hands into the wall, keeping your entire body straight and your back flat. Exhale through your mouth as you push away; then inhale through your nose as you come toward the wall (see Figure 8-15).

Build up to 3 sets of 15 reps with a ninety-second rest between sets. When you can do these perfectly, begin Knee Push-Ups on the next workout.

FIGURE 8-15

Knee Push-Up

Lie facedown on a mat or soft carpet. Bend your knees, and raise your feet. Place your hands on the floor just outside your shoulders, with the fingertips at chin level. Keep your head in neutral position. Push into the floor and lift your body until your elbows are fully extended (see Figure 8-16). Lower your body until your chest touches the floor (see Figure 8-17); then push up again.

You come up the moment your chest touches the floor—you don't rest there.

If you like, you can cross your ankles in the air.

Do 3 sets of 6 reps with a ninety-second rest between sets. Add 1 to 2 reps every workout until you build up to 3 sets of 15 reps with ninety-second rests. When you can do 15 reps perfectly, move on to Standard Push-Ups.

FIGURE 8-16

FIGURE 8-17

Standard Push-Up

S ince women generally have less upper body strength than men, I give different rep ranges for each.

Because you should never begin a strenuous activity before warming up the specific part of the body that will be working hard, you must warm up before beginning these push-ups.

Do 1 set of 8 reps of Knee Push-Ups as a warm-up; then rest sixty seconds.

Take the same position as for Knee Push-Ups, except come up on the pads of your toes. Keep your legs straight, clench your buttocks, and push yourself up (see Figure 8-18). Lower your body until your chest touches the floor (see Figure 8-19); then push up again.

Here's your goal for Standard Push-Ups: your back should be as straight as a broomstick, from your tailbone to the back of your skull. Avoid arching, twisting, or humping the back.

FIGURE 8-18

FIGURE 8-19

Women do 3 sets of 6 reps and build up to 3 sets of 8 with ninety-second rests. Men start with 3 sets of 6 reps and build up to 3 sets of 12 with ninety-second rests.

When you can do the highest number of reps perfectly, move on to Raised-Foot Push-Ups.

Raised-Foot Push-Up

These are exactly the same as Standard Push-Ups, except that your feet are up on a support. Adding height increases the amount of weight bearing down on your hands (resistance) by 15 to 20 percent—a substantial amount. Push-ups done this way may look like Standard Push-Ups, but they're far more difficult. I've included them in Phase 1 to enable you to manage the Ballistic Push-Ups in Phase 2, which are even harder.

You must rest longer to complete all three sets. Two minutes is absolutely necessary.

A good starting height for your support is 6 inches.

Do 1 set of 8 Knee Push-Ups as a warm-up; then rest sixty seconds.

Do the Raised-Foot Push-Ups the same way you do the Standard Push-Ups, with a speed of one and a half seconds going up and two seconds going down (see Figures 8-20 and 8-21).

Men begin with 3 sets of 6 reps and build up to 12 reps with a two-minute rest between sets.

Women begin with 3 sets of 5 reps with a two-minute rest and try to build up to 8 reps—but if you can do 6 of these, you're in excellent shape!

You can take this exercise even further by raising the support to about 15 inches, which is really challenging. At each progression, reset your reps back to 5.

Caution: *never do fewer than 5 reps, and never hold your breath while doing Raised-Foot Push-Ups. If you do, you may get dizzy or even pass out.*

FIGURE 8-20

FIGURE 8-21

PHASE 1: BUILDING LEAN MUSCLE
SET B: LOWER BODY

Air Squat

This extremely practical exercise develops strength in the buttocks, the quadriceps, and to some extent in the lower back. You'll be able to bound upstairs or hike uphill more easily. Men: it will make you better lovers because it develops the muscles you use to thrust. Frail or stiff people will be able to stand up out of a chair more easily. And one other very pleasant change occurs: you get a nice rounded backside.

Stand with your feet hip width apart; then move each foot 2 inches farther out and turn it out 30 degrees. Your arms are comfortably by your sides, and your head is in neutral position.

If you aren't flexible enough to stand this way, you need to do the Inner Thigh, Hip Flexor, Buttocks Muscle, and Calf Muscle stretches to release tight hip and leg muscles before doing this exercise.

Begin to squat down. As your body lowers, raise both arms to shoulder level, parallel to the floor, with palms facing down. Ideally, come down until your thighs are parallel to the floor. Your torso should lean slightly forward, but no more than 30 degrees (see Figure 8-22).

If you can't lower yourself far enough, spend a couple of days doing the four stretches mentioned earlier.

If you lean too far forward, you're not doing a squat—you're working your lower back, not your quads.

Come up to standing position with energy and intent! Drive your feet into the floor, contracting your buttocks vigorously, and push yourself up forcefully.

Remember, you need this level of energy to develop the muscle fibers that build lean muscle. Put some feeling into it!

I give my trainees this image: pretend there's a book on your head, and do the whole set looking straight ahead with your head perfectly level to keep that book from toppling off.

Inhale through your nose as you drop into the squat. Exhale as you come up, puffing out your cheeks and blowing out forcefully through pursed lips.

Your tempo should be approximately 2 seconds going down and 1.5 seconds coming up.

If you're tall, it takes longer to go down and up, and if you're shorter, it takes less time, so you may need to adjust these times somewhat.

Since the last thing you want to do is strengthen a dysfunctional movement pattern,

FIGURE 8-22

it's best to do Air Squats in front of a mirror so you can correct your form. Many people either ascend or descend bearing more weight on one leg. Check whether your hips swerve to one side as you raise or lower your body. This is a sure sign of unequal weight-bearing. Most often you can easily fix it by consciously putting more weight on the other side. If your body can't follow this mental command, you have a physical restriction that must be corrected. Do the Buttocks Muscle, Human Pinwheel, Inner Thigh, Calf Muscle, Long Thigh, Hamstring, and Hip Flexor stretches. Pick the three tightest muscles based on how hard it is to do these stretches. Then do the stretches for those muscles for a week. Once the muscles are released, your squats will be balanced and symmetrical, reducing your risk of injury.

If you're out of condition, start with 3 sets of 6 reps. If you're fairly strong, start with 10 reps. Rest for ninety seconds in between sets. To progress, add 1 to 2 reps at each workout, building up to 20.

This is a tough exercise and can be quite challenging as the reps increase. But by the end of six weeks, 20 reps should be as easy as 6 were when you started.

Split Squats

Like Air Squats, Split Squats are very functional. On the front leg side, they develop the quads and the gluteus muscles to stabilize the hip—meaning, they improve your balance. On the rear leg side, they stretch the hip flexor and train the gluteus and hip rotators neurologically to stabilize the hip. The wobbling you experience when doing Split Squats is actually your friend. Balance is crucial for everyday functioning, so we want the balance challenge that this exercise offers. If you're a runner—especially a sprinter—a basketball or soccer player, or a ballet dancer, Split Squats are great for you.

You begin by finding how far apart your feet should be when you're in the squat. This distance differs for everyone, so you have to experiment.

Regular Split Squat

Stand with your feet under your hips (for most people, about 6 inches apart) and your hands on your hips. Step your right leg forward about 15 inches and then continue to move it forward in increments of several inches at a time, bending the right knee, until you feel a moderate stretch in the front of the left hip.

This is your starting distance. As your flexibility improves over your first six or so sessions, your starting distance will increase slightly with each session. Then you'll reach a point where it stops increasing, and it feels pretty good. That's your true starting distance.

With your hands still on your hips, straighten your torso so it's upright. Bend your right knee down and forward while allowing the left (rear) knee to bend comfortably (see Figure 8-23).

The rear knee bends to help the forward knee bend. Most people keep the rear leg too straight. Remember to bend it. You must be up on the ball of the rear foot with the heel raised.

If you find that you can't get into position at all and keep tipping over, do the Hip Flexor, Inner Thigh, Sole-of-Foot, and Human Pinwheel stretches to release your hips, and the Low Back Stretch to improve your balance. Then try the Split Squat again.

If you can't bend the front knee a full 90 degrees, don't worry—by the sixth week, it'll be there. Meanwhile, just bend it as much as you can.

If you can get into position but have poor balance, put one hand on a table nearby as you do the squat. The challenge is to let go of the table as soon as you can.

Now begin the actual squat. Bend both knees so your body lowers as much as possible; then straighten your knees and come up. Keep your back as straight as possible, with the intent of being perfectly straight. Your head is in neutral position (see Figure 8-24). Exhale as you come up, using forceful, intentional breathing.

The front knee should come no farther forward than your toe when it bends. The back knee bends just enough to enable the front knee to bend. Remember that you're on the ball of your rear foot—the heel is not on the floor.

Remember not to breathe with your mouth open! Purse your lips and blow out forcefully on the exhale.

Imagine having that book on the top of your head—don't let it drop.

Beginners and frail people, expect to lose your balance frequently. Take this as your challenge, and free yourself of that table as soon as possible.

FIGURE 8-23

If you are not very strong, do 3 sets of 5 reps, alternating sides, with a forty-five-second rest period after each side. Stronger people do 8 reps. The goal for both is 15 reps.

Your tempo is one and a half seconds up and two seconds down.

FIGURE 8-24

Split Squat with Weights

Once you can do 3 sets of 15 perfect reps of Regular Split Squats—no wobbling—you've earned the right to do them holding weights. Doing Split Squats this way builds the strength you need to do the Lunges in Phase 2, which make a much greater demand on your muscles. Use your lighter pair of dumbbells or two plastic jugs. If you have two kettlebells of the same weight, you can use them.

FIGURE 8-25

Hold a weight in each hand, and take the same position as for Regular Split Squats, except that instead of having your hands on your hips, your arms are down (see Figure 8-25).

You aren't lifting the weights, but you are gripping them firmly.

Do 3 sets of 5 reps, with a forty-five-second rest between sides.

If you can't do 5 reps, the weight is too heavy. If the 4th or 5th rep is difficult, rest thirty seconds longer—it will make your next two sets much easier.

Overhead Squat

This difficult but extremely powerful exercise works the spine, low back, buttocks, abdominal muscles, and quads—it's the ultimate core exercise. My definition of the core is the part of the body between the navel and the upper thighs; for good daily functioning, it must be strong. The Overhead Squat coordinates the muscles of the core and torso and is one of the best ways to improve posture. It's also one of the few exercises that connects the upper and lower body, working both in a beautifully concerted way. This squat requires a great deal of mental energy and focus, but if you master it, your back will be super strong and you'll have fantastic balance, flexibility, and posture.

You need a broomstick, mop handle, or what is called a body bar, which is weighted and gives a greater strengthening effect. I recommend a 9-pound bar as a good starting point for most people. If you have an adjustable Olympic bar (a heavier bar that is the standard size used in competitions), you can use that. Make sure you use collars so the plates don't fall off. **Note:** anyone who has never done this exercise before—including experienced weight lifters—should practice with a mop handle or similar stick before using any weighted bar. Once you can hold the mop handle at the correct point above your head *and* do 10 reps in perfect form, you can move on to using a weighted bar.

Begin by determining the correct width for your hand grip.

Hold the bar with each hand 12 inches beyond the hip on that side. Stand with your feet about 4 inches wider than hip width and turned out 45 degrees.

If your hips are tight and your balance poor, your stance can be wider with your feet turned out more. As you become more flexible, progressively narrow your stance until your feet are 4 inches wider than your hips and turned out 30 degrees. Be aware, however, that this is an ideal to strive for; it requires great flexibility in the buttocks and calves, and except for professional dancers, most people can't actually get there.

Hold the bar in front of you, with the backs of your hands facing away from you. Raise your arms overhead and as far back as possible, with elbows straight, and then lower them. Narrow your grip by an inch on both sides, and lift the bar again. Your ability to move the bar backward above your head decreases a little. Keep decreasing your grip by ½ to 1 inch at

FIGURE 8-26

a time until you cannot easily move the bar to a point 2 inches behind the center of your head. This is your grip width.

As long as the bar can go farther than this point, your grip is too wide. If your shoulders are very tight, you may need to use an extremely wide grip just to bring the bar to this point. Everyone is different, so you may need to adjust the point itself slightly to keep your balance.

Now begin the actual squat. Lift the bar to shoulder level; then press it above your head (watch out for your chin). Your wrists should be bent backward, so you're holding the bar mainly in the meat of your palms. Holding the bar above your head, grip it very firmly with intention.

Make sure that the bar is not just sitting in your palms. To develop power and strength, you want to create real tension in your arms. For most people, the bar should come approximately 2 inches behind the center of the head. However, the center of balance is different for everyone. Experiment to find your own balance point.

Caution: don't hold the bar too far back or you may tip backward. Similarly, to protect your lower back, be sure the bar does not come in front of your head while you are squatting.

If you're not very flexible, or you feel wobbly, put a chair behind you to fall back into if you lose your balance. The chair also provides a psychological sense of safety—you'll find you can squat down farther because you know it's there.

If your Achilles tendons are tight, use supports to lift your heels about 1 inch. Two thin books work well, as does a prop like a yoga wedge.

Keeping your elbows as straight as you can, shrug your shoulders up, bringing the tips of the shoulders toward your ears (see Figure 8-26).

This action makes the bar more stable. You feel more solid, energetic, and balanced when you hold it this way.

Bend both knees so your body lowers as much as possible (see Figure 8-27); then straighten your knees and come up. Keep your back as straight as possible. Your head is in neutral. Exhale as you come up, using forceful, intentional breathing.

If you have shoulder problems, do the Chest Muscle, Front-of-Shoulder, and Biceps stretches. They should enable you to raise your arms comfortably.

If you find it difficult to get into the squat position, your spine muscles may be weak. Do these stretches: Holding a Small Globe, Hip Flexor, Human Pinwheel, Buttocks Muscle, Inner Thigh Spectrum, and Calf Muscle. Pick the three that represent the tightest muscles, and do these stretches for a week. This greatly improves your Overhead Squat technique.

FIGURE 8-27

As you grow more flexible and coordinated, aggressively narrow your stance and turn your feet outward less. At the same time, your grip will narrow.

Your tempo should be two and a half seconds down and then two seconds up.

Many people tend to bring their arms forward when they're in the down position. Remember to keep your arms between the point 1 inch behind the center of your head and another point at the back of your head, but never bring them behind your head.

Women begin with 3 sets of 5 reps, and men do 8 reps. Both take a ninety-second rest period between sets and add 1 rep per workout, increasing to 12 reps.

The need for balance and coordination makes the Overhead Squat extremely challenging, so the rep ranges are lower. To go to the next level, you don't need to increase your reps past 12; it's better to decrease your rest period to seventy-five seconds and then sixty seconds. Once you can do 12 reps with a forty-five-second rest, increase the downstroke to three seconds while keeping the upstroke at two seconds. That may not seem like much—but try it.

Am I Ready for Phase 2?

The Phase 1 training offers both strength gains and visual improvements, and these are your criteria for deciding when you're ready to progress to Phase 2. **Note:** decreasing your rest periods in Phase 1 before moving to Phase 2 is optional, but I recommend it because it will make the transition to Phase 2 more seamless.

First, you'll notice that you have more energy and get less tired during the day. You find yourself bounding up stairs more easily. You discover that it's much easier to pick up a child or a heavy bag of groceries. Once you see these changes, you know you've got lots of lean muscle. At the same time, your mood improves, and your food actually tastes better. Believe it or not, these are clear signs that you've gained a lot of lean tissue.

Your body also gives you visual clues. Men find that their shoulders are broader, their abdomen flatter, and their waist narrower. They feel taller because their posture is more upright. Their muscles are more robust, with hints of veins appearing as body fat decreases. They see their cheekbones emerging as their face muscles are toned. Women see less body fat, improved posture, perked-up buttocks, and a narrower waist. In fact they look smaller all over, as lean muscle replaces fat.

PHASE 2: BUILDING EXPLOSIVE STRENGTH
SET A: UPPER BODY

Two-Arm Swing

The Two-Arm Swing, a more advanced version of the Dead Lift, forces you to move the weight rapidly. It enables your body to command its muscles to fire explosively to perform the actions needed in everyday life. Even an older or frail person can do this exercise and get huge benefits by using an appropriate weight and following the Kaizen principle of progressing in very small increments.

The Two-Arm Swing works the hamstrings, buttocks, and lower back. Even though the arms move rapidly, the shoulder muscles are only minimally involved; the meat of the exercise is in its effect on your core. It's the first explosive exercise you'll be doing, and you need to understand that *explosive* means "sudden and forceful." This and all the other

Phase 2 exercises must be performed with speed and vigor. Reaching your goal for this part of the program depends on it.

This exercise is actually pretty easy both to learn and to perform, but it may seem daunting if you're not used to lifting rapidly. I've seen a five-foot-two, 110-pound woman athlete do 25 perfect reps with a 20-kilogram kettlebell (44 pounds). If she could swing that weight, anyone reading this book can do fewer reps, swinging five or six times less weight. Within three or four sessions, you should feel quite comfortable.

Start with your lighter weight.

Caution: if you have arthritic hands without strength, don't do this exercise. You must have an adequate grip or the weight will go flying.

Stand with your feet 2 inches wider than hip width on each side and turned out 30 degrees. Place the weight in front of you so that when you look down, the tips of your toes are in line with the middle of it.

This position puts the weight right under your center of gravity. A common mistake is to stand 10 inches away from the weight and lean forward. This will hurt your back. Make sure you're right up against the weight.

Keeping your back flat, bend your knees and grab the weight with both hands (see Figure 8-28). Then come to standing position, letting your arms hang. To swing the weight, bend forward at the hip with a flat back and bent knees, squeeze your buttocks, and straighten your knees to thrust your hips vigorously forward and give the swing an explosive momentum (see Figure 8-29). *Even if you're already a weight lifter*, start with 2 short reps to warm up. The first swing should go to chest level and the second to the top of your head. On the third swing, bring the weight to an almost-vertical position (see Figure 8-30).

Don't bring the weight to a completely vertical position. If you do, it might flip backward. You don't want it to go behind your head.

If you've never done this type of exercise, use the Kaizen principle and start small. For your first session, swing only as high as your chest for all three sets. In the next workout, take the weight as high as the top of your head. Then in the third, swing to the almost-vertical position—but keep doing the 2 warm-up reps before the first set.

To come down, let the weight do a free fall, controlling its speed as it nears bottom just enough to be able to raise it again.

Most people tend at first to slow the descent of the weight. But you really need to let it fall. If you're not used to high speed,

FIGURE 8-28   **FIGURE 8-29**   **FIGURE 8-30**

this may seem scary, but I promise you that after a couple of sets it will feel totally natural and easy—like being a child on a swing.

Intentional breathing is crucial in this exercise. On the downstroke, inhale. On the upswing, do a forced expiration. The expiration should be completed as the weight reaches almost vertical.

Breathing must be rhythmic: people sometimes skip a rep, so be sure you take a new breath with every rep.

Remember that you need to scrunch up your face and blow out hard. (I find that women in particular sometimes don't like to do this.) But you must breathe aggressively to make the exercise work.

Start with 6 reps. Do not include the 2 partial reps in that total, although you must do them in every single workout. If you can, increase your reps by 1 to 2 in every workout. Your goal is 20 reps. Once you can comfortably do 3 sets of 20 with a ninety-second rest between sets for a couple of workouts, decrease your rest period to seventy-five seconds, then sixty seconds.

When you reach 20 reps with a sixty-second rest, switch to your heavier weight and reset your reps down to 6. Then slowly build up to 20 again. Once you're at 20 reps with this shorter rest period, you're there!

Important points to remember:
> *The crucial aspect of the Two-Arm Swing is speed: that's what makes it ballistic. Aim for acceleration on the way up, and let the weight drop on the way down, decelerating as it nears bottom. As you grow more comfortable with this exercise, you'll find yourself speeding up naturally.*

> *Another critical point: your arms do almost nothing in this exercise. Most of the momentum comes from thrusting your hips. Your shoulders barely lift the weight. Your arms are there basically to prevent it from shooting off into space. Keep them straight throughout the exercise.*

> *As the previous point indicates, this exercise is about using your core muscles to thrust your hips. It requires rapid, vigorous contraction. If you slow down, the exercise loses its value.*

> *Be careful not to overshoot at the top of the swing. You don't want the weight to flip back over your wrist. Until you become sure of your strength and timing, shoot for lifting it 2 to 3 inches short of vertical.*

Clean and Press

Clean means lifting the weight from the floor to shoulder level. This exercise gives you a lot of bang for the buck. If I had to choose just one exercise to do, this would be it. The Clean and Press develops balance and coordination. It works the abdominal muscles, hamstrings, quads, buttocks, lower back, shoulders, rotator cuff, and triceps.

Because the Clean and Press is what I call a high-displacement exercise, meaning that the weight is lifted over a great distance (floor to overhead), you do fewer reps. Since it makes greater demands on the body than most exercises, it requires a particularly powerful intention to reap the benefits. You must get your head in there and do it with laserlike concentration, passion, and focus. In addition, since this exercise requires explosive movement in a bent-over posture, you must be thoroughly warmed up before you begin.

Start with your lighter weight.

Stand with your feet 2 inches wider than hip width on each side and turned out 30 degrees. Place the weight next to your right foot. Your left

FIGURE 8-31

FIGURE 8-32

arm is out to the side, acting as a counterbalance. Bend from the hips with bent knees and a flat back. Keep your head in neutral; your eyes look down to grab the weight, but your head doesn't move (see Figure 8-31). Pick up the weight and, in one explosive motion, snap it up to shoulder level (see Figure 8-32).

If you're using a kettlebell, it will swing over your wrist onto the back of your forearm. It may seem likely to sprain your wrist, but with a bit of practice you'll find the right amount of force to use so it won't hurt you. To begin, use just moderate speed so you don't flip it too hard. Even so, kettlebell beginners often bang their forearms a bit. For this reason, I recommend starting with a dumbbell for at least six sessions, if possible, to learn the gross movements and get comfortable with the exercise overall. Then, when you start using the kettlebell, you can focus just on the wrist.

When the weight is heavy, the "clean" often includes a hop, a natural movement that happens as part of the effort of lifting. Some people lift the entire foot off the floor when they hop. Others just come up onto their toes.

FIGURE 8-33

Once the weight is at your shoulder, turn your hand 45 degrees so the palm faces diagonally left and bend your knees slightly. Then straighten your knees and, gripping the weight tightly, push it up strongly to the ceiling until your arm is straight (see Figure 8-33).

Hold the weight at your farthest reach for half a second, lower it to your shoulder, and then flip it down, using a rapid forward roll of your shoulder and a rapid forward flip of the wrist so the weight comes down to about knee level (see Figure 8-34). Come back up to standing upright (see Figure 8-35); then lower the weight to 6 inches above the floor. From here, repeat the Clean and Press.

FIGURE 8-34   **FIGURE 8-35**

Start with 5 reps, and build up to 10 with a forty-five-second rest. Switch arms with each set. When you can comfortably do 3 sets of 12 reps on each side, reduce your rest period to thirty seconds. Once you're doing 3 sets of 12 reps with a thirty-second rest, switch to your heavier weight, reset your reps to 5, and start building up all over again. Your goal is 3 sets of 12 reps on each side with a thirty-second rest.

Ballistic Push-Up

These are the same as the Raised-Foot Push-Ups in Phase 1, but you do them faster and with more intense focus. Adjusting your speed and intention leads to vastly different outcomes, giving you far more power and strength. Begin with a support about 6 inches high. The more resistance you use, the more fast-twitch (strength-promoting) muscle fibers you develop.

Start with a warm-up of 1 set of 8 Knee Push-Ups.

Women do 3 sets of 5 reps with a two-minute rest between sets. Build up to 8 reps. Your upstroke is a half second and your downstroke is two seconds. When you reach 8 reps, slow your downstroke to three seconds.

If you like, you can progress further by decreasing your rest period to ninety seconds and then sixty seconds. That's your ultimate goal.

Men start with 3 sets of 6 reps with a ninety-second rest between sets. Your upstroke is a half second and your downstroke is two seconds. Build up to 3 sets of 10 reps; then slow your downstroke to three seconds.

If you like, you can progress by decreasing the rest period to ninety seconds and then sixty seconds. That's your ultimate goal, and if you can reach it, you are really strong. You've reached push-up nirvana and need not go any further.

Reaching ultimate goals for Ballistic Push-Ups requires intentional breathing; blow out air as you push up. As the set progresses, you fatigue and your speed slows. That doesn't matter. The important thing is to maintain the intent to do the high-speed contractions. If your brain intends to push harder and faster, you engage many more fibers—even if you don't actually speed up that much—and gain the strength you seek.

PHASE 2: BUILDING EXPLOSIVE STRENGTH
SET B: LOWER BODY

Speed Squat

Again, Speed Squats are the same as the Air Squats in Phase 1, except much faster. This is a tough exercise, but if you do the regular Air Squats for six weeks, you should be in shape for Speed Squats.

You must be completely warmed up before doing Speed Squats. Do 1 set of 8 Air Squats at normal speed to warm up. Make sure you're sweaty! Rest for sixty seconds.

Now begin doing squats at high speed, using intentional breathing, aiming for 10 reps in twenty seconds. When this feels comfortable and smooth, and your form is absolutely perfect, start increasing your reps, adding 1 to 2 reps every workout. Your ultimate goal is 20 reps in twenty-five seconds.

After 3 sets, rest for ninety seconds, and move on to the Lunges.

These squats require balance and coordination—including coordinating your breathing with your movements, exhaling explosively as you come up. Don't be surprised if you're tired when you finish.

Moving at such high speed, it's easy to lose your balance. If you're not used to high-speed exercise, start with 5 reps in ten to twelve seconds and slowly build to 20 in twenty-five seconds by the end of the sixth week. If you feel insecure about falling backward, put a chair behind you.

If you wobble too much or you get hip pain or clicking, popping, or grinding in your knees, don't do this exercise yet. Do the following stretches: Holding a Large Globe, Low Back, Hip Flexor, Long Inner Thigh, Calf Muscle, and Long Quad. Pick the two or three stretches that are hardest, and do them every day for a week. The squats will then be much easier.

Lunges

The Split Squats in Phase 1 were the preparation for the Lunges, which require more balance, coordination, and explosive strength. The benefits are the same as for the Split Squats, but the Lunges also stimulate the fast-twitch fibers, giving you explosive strength.

Do the 30-Degree Lunges in the same workout session, right after the Straight Lunges. Do not alternate legs within a set. If you alternate legs, you rest each leg after every rep and are less efficient in building explosive strength.

Straight Lunge

Stand with your feet hip width apart and your hands on your hips. Step your right foot forward in one movement to the same distance that you used for the Split Squats, and then step back (see Figure 8-36). Your left knee bends enough to accommodate the movement. Use intentional breathing, inhaling as you lunge forward, blowing out the air on the exertion as you step back.

If you feel a little insecure, shorten the distance somewhat, but strive to reach your previous distance as soon as you can.

FIGURE 8-36

If you're not very strong, start with 2 sets of 5 reps with a sixty-second rest period after each leg. At 8 reps, reduce your rest period to forty-five seconds.

Stronger people start with 2 sets of 8 reps and a forty-five-second rest. Add 1 to 2 reps per workout, building up to 2 sets of 12 reps.

You should be able to do the Straight Lunges quite well after three sessions. If that doesn't happen—if you find that your balance is poor and you land in a different spot each time you lunge—you need to stop and do the Hamstring, Human Pinwheel, Inner Thigh, Buttocks, Sole-of-Foot, and Hip Flexor stretches, plus the Low Back Stretch. As before, pick the three hardest and do those for about a week.

Do not *continue lunging with poor technique; it's a surefire way to injure yourself. Try this experiment: do two or three of these stretches, and then try the lunge again. I guarantee your form will be much better. But don't start doing it as a regular exercise until you've spent that week releasing your hip and leg muscles with the stretches.*

30-Degree Lunge

Once you've become very proficient in the Straight Lunge, you can get fancy and add this side lunge. Your forward leg simply steps out 30 degrees to the side instead of straight ahead (see Figure 8-37).

The 30-Degree Lunge trains the inner thigh muscles more effectively. In addition, changing the angle adds another element of balance challenge—something you always want.

If you're not very strong, start with 2 sets of 5 reps with a sixty-second rest period. Add 1 to 2 reps per workout, and at 8 reps, reduce your rest to forty-five seconds.

Stronger people start with 2 sets of 8 reps with a forty-five-second rest and add 1 to 2 reps per workout.

Both groups build up to 2 sets of 12 reps. At this point, reduce your rest period to thirty seconds.

FIGURE 8-37

Lunge with Dumbbells

When you can do 2 sets of 12 reps of both Straight and 30-Degree Lunges in perfect form, increase the resistance by holding dumbbells during both types. Start with your lighter weight and set your reps back to 5, build up again to 12 reps, and then reset with your heavier weights. When you can do 2 sets of 12 reps with your heavier weights, you're where you want to be.

Overhead Squat with Additional Weight

This is not an explosive exercise, but it's extremely valuable for maintaining overall conditioning: it blends upper and lower body strength, plus improves posture.

This exercise is similar to the Overhead Squats in Phase 1, except that you make sure your thighs are completely parallel to the ground. Also, you use either increased weight or more reps with a different tempo. Ideally, buy a weighted body bar (I recommend 12 pounds, even for small people), or use an Olympic bar and add weights to the point where you can comfortably do 2 sets of 5 reps, with the 5th rep being slightly difficult.

Do the same Overhead Squat as in Phase 1 at a tempo of two and a half seconds down and two seconds up, using your increased weight. On the downstroke, make sure your thighs are really parallel to the ground. If you can, go down even farther, so that your hips are slightly lower than your knees (making your thighs below parallel).

Many people tend to bring their arms forward when they're in the down position. Remember to keep your arms between the point 1 inch behind the center of your head and another point at the back of your head, but never behind your head.

Once you can do this comfortably, narrow your stance by 1 inch on each side and turn your feet in slightly. Change your tempo to 3 seconds down and 1 second up. Start at 2 sets of 5 reps with a ninety-second rest; then add 1 rep in each workout until you reach 12 reps. At this point decrease the rest period to sixty seconds, and add a 3rd set of 12 reps.

If you don't want to buy a weighted bar, do the exercise as described with your broomstick. This does not add strength, but it ensures the preservation of lean tissue and gives you great posture and flexibility. Do at least 2 sets of 12 reps each.

Now That You've Reached Your Goal . . .

You naturally want to maintain your wonderful new state of health and well-being. That requires keeping up your three workout sessions a week—amounting to just an hour total—plus keeping up your stretching.

After you complete Phase 2, begin to alternate the Phase 1 and 2 workouts: four weeks of one, then four weeks of the other. If you do only one type of training, your body accommodates to it and becomes stale. You need to flip-flop between slower-speed and high-speed workouts.

And *never stop stretching*. Now that you're pain free, you can maintain healthy fascia by doing the healthy person program in Chapter 9. Ideally, do the three fascial stretches in this program at the end of a workout, when your body is really warm—they'll be far more effective.

If ever you feel a twinge, you can switch in the specific stretches for your pain problem—or check the other pain programs if you develop any new symptoms.

If you've worked through my entire strengthening program, you are definitely at a level of strength and functioning that will keep you permanently pain free. Now you have a choice. Mine would be to buy heavier weights and reset my reps lower, so I could build up even more strength. (In my book, you can never be too strong.) But if you choose to stay where you are, you'll still be in excellent shape—by anyone's yardstick.

CHAPTER NINE

Your Personal Program

Choosing the Stretches You Need

T his chapter is a how-to manual for fixing your own body. It presents programs for treating nine specific pain conditions. Even after you fix any problem you have now, you can consult this chapter if ever a new problem develops, and do the stretches to fix that problem.

The chapter also offers two general programs for preventing and relieving problems commonly experienced by office workers and elderly people, as well as a healthy person program designed to keep anyone without a pain problem from getting one.

General Instructions

As you work through the program you've chosen, follow these guidelines:

> Always stretch both sides of the body, because the side where you don't have pain still contributes to the problem in some way.
> For the Inner Thigh and Hamstring spectrums, do all three stretches, pick the tightest muscle on each side, and then stretch that one, as described in the instructions for those stretches in Chapter 7. If you're not sure which muscle is tightest, do the Middle Hamstring and General Inner Thigh stretches.
> Remember that it's preferable to do the spinal stretches just before bed. You can do the fascial stretches and self-therapy techniques anytime you like, as long as your body is warm.
> For best results, apply Traumeel (see Chapter 10) to painful muscles after stretching (for joints, use Zeel). You can also take systemic enzymes and joint health supplements (for fast results, I recommend the product Joint Support—see page 67).

How to Progress

Fixing certain pain conditions requires quite a few stretches. To keep your stretch program to fifteen minutes a day, I've limited the programs to six stretches at any one time but designed them so that once you can do a given stretch well, you progress to a new one. The arrows in the programs indicate the progressions. For example, in the program for neck pain, you begin with Dead Roach 1, Holding a Small Globe, Side-of-Neck Stretch, Chest Muscle Stretch, and Hip Flexor Stretch. Once you can do Dead Roach 1 correctly, according to the criteria for spinal stretches in the following list, stop doing that stretch and begin doing Dead Roach 2. When you can do Holding a Small Globe according to the criteria, move to the Low Back Stretch, and so on. Stretches that are more difficult for you will take longer to get right. So you may find yourself still doing Holding a Small Globe and

Hip Flexor Stretch, say, even though you've progressed to Dead Roach 2, Shrug Muscle Stretch, and Biceps Stretch.

Here's how to tell when to progress:

> **Spinal stretches:** when you can hold a stretch for sixty seconds with perfect form and almost no shaking, you're ready to move to the next one.
> **Fascial stretches in which you stretch one side at a time:** it's usually much harder to do a stretch on one side than on the other. When this dysfunctional side can do the stretch almost as well as the other side, it's time to move to the next stretch listed (sometimes this is not a stretch, but a self-therapy technique from Chapter 10).
> **Wrist and forearm stretches:** once you can press the entire palm flat (inner stretch) or the entire back of the hand flat (outer stretch) using moderate pressure and with your forearm perpendicular to your hand, move to the next stretch listed.

Specific Conditions

The programs that follow address the most common pain problems that bring people to a therapist. They cover 90 percent of all the causes of pain that most people encounter.

Neck Pain

Use this program for pain right underneath the place where the back of the skull meets the neck, and for migraines, jaw pain (TMJ), and pain on the side of the neck. I've included the Hip Flexor Stretch here because it straightens your posture, bringing your head over the center of the body so the back of your neck doesn't have to work as hard.

> Dead Roach 1 (page 90) → Dead Roach 2 (page 93)
> Holding a Small Globe (page 98) → Low Back Stretch (page 104)
> Side-of-Neck Stretch (page 115) → Shrug Muscle Stretch (page 122)

> Chest Muscle Stretch (page 127) → Biceps Stretch (page 129)
> Hip Flexor Stretch (page 136) → Hamstring Spectrum (page 157)

Shoulder Pain (Rotator Cuff Problems, Tendonitis)

Since the shoulder makes every movement known to humankind, this program is a bit complex.

> Dead Roach 1 (page 90)
> Dead Roach 2 (page 93)
> Side-of-Neck Stretch (page 115) → Shrug Muscle Stretch (page 122)
> Front-of-Shoulder Stretch (page 117) → Chest Muscle Stretch (page 127) → Biceps Stretch (page 129)
> Broad Back Stretch (page 125) → Triceps Stretch (page 131)
> Deep Shoulder Stretch 2 (page 120) → Deep Shoulder Stretch 1 (page 119)

Elbow Pain (Including Tennis and Golfer's Elbow)

Like carpal tunnel syndrome, elbow pain is frequently misdiagnosed as originating in the area where the pain is. In fact, it invariably arises from the neck and the front of the shoulder. Therefore, you relieve it by releasing those areas. Instead of using a compression strap, try these stretches—they will fix the problem instead of just masking symptoms.

> Dead Roach 2 (page 93) → Steeple (page 96)
> Side-of-Neck Stretch (page 115) → Shrug Muscle Stretch (page 122)
> Chest Muscle Stretch (page 127) → Biceps Stretch (page 129)
> Triceps Stretch (page 131)
> Inside-of-Forearm Stretch (page 133) → Palm Release (page 232)
> Outside-of-Forearm Stretch (page 135)

Carpal Tunnel Syndrome and Hand Pain

In my twenty years of practice, I've yet to see a true carpal tunnel syndrome—that is, one in which the problem is located entirely in the wrist.

Instead, I see the pain originating from muscles in the neck, armpit, forearm, biceps, and chest. Accordingly, this program is designed to release those parts of the body. It also relieves arthritic hand pain.

> Dead Roach 2 (page 93) → Steeple (page 96)
> Holding a Small Globe (page 98)
> Side-of-Neck Stretch (page 115) → Shrug Muscle Stretch (page 122)
> Front-of-Shoulder Stretch (page 117) → Chest Muscle Stretch (page 127) → Biceps Stretch (page 129)
> Inside-of-Forearm Stretch (page 133) → Palm Release (page 232)
> Outside-of-Forearm Stretch (page 135)

Mid- and Upper-Back Pain

Many people have pain located between the shoulder blades and a few inches below, which goes hand-in-hand with neck pain. This program relieves it.

> Steeple (page 96)
> Holding a Small Globe (page 98)
> Broad Back Stretch (page 125)
> Mid-Back Stretch (page 123)
> Chest Muscle Stretch (page 127)
> Hip Flexor Stretch (page 136) → Hamstring Spectrum (page 157)

Lower-Back Pain and Sciatica

This program relieves both lower-back pain and sciatica, which are caused by similar fascial restrictions. **Caution:** if you have active, painful sciatica, do not do the Low Back Stretch and Hamstring Spectrum until the inflammation has subsided.

> Low Back Stretch (page 104) → Holding a Large Globe (page 101)
> Hip Flexor Stretch (page 136) → Long Quad Stretch (page 141)
> Human Pinwheel (page 145)

> Hamstring Spectrum (page 157)
> Buttocks Muscle Stretch (page 143)
> Inner Thigh Spectrum (page 150)

Hip Pain

Do these stretches to relieve pain in the front or side of the hip that causes you to limp when you walk. And if you have trouble getting out of cabs or low chairs, this program makes a big difference.

> Holding a Large Globe (page 101)
> Low Back Stretch (page 104)
> Hip Flexor Stretch (page 136) → Long Quad Stretch (page 141)
> Inner Thigh Spectrum (page 150)
> Buttocks Muscle Stretch (page 143) → Human Pinwheel (page 145) → IT Band Release (page 230)
> Hamstring Spectrum (page 157)

Knee Pain

This program relieves pain under the kneecap, clicking and popping, generalized soreness around the knee, and instability (i.e., you can't run or move sideways without pain).

Do not use a compression strap for knee pain! It gives you symptomatic relief but doesn't fix the problem. If used long term, it can hurt you by forcing the muscles whose injury caused the pain initially to keep working.

> Holding a Large Globe (page 101)
> Low Back Stretch (page 104)
> Hip Flexor Stretch (page 136) → Long Quad Stretch (page 141)
> Buttocks Muscle Stretch (page 143) → Human Pinwheel (page 145)
> Hamstring Spectrum (page 157) → Long Inner Thigh Stretch (page 155) → Calf Muscle Stretch (page 161)
> Quadriceps Release (page 233) → IT Band Release (page 230)

Foot and Ankle Pain

This program relieves a variety of foot and ankle problems, including plantar fasciitis.

> Low Back Stretch (page 104)
> Hamstring Spectrum (page 157) → Human Pinwheel (page 145) → Buttocks Muscle Stretch (page 143)
> Calf Muscle Stretch (page 161)
> Shin Muscle Stretch (page 164)
> Sole-of-Foot Stretch (page 166)
> Sole-of-Foot Release (page 228)

General Programs

It's always more effective to catch and correct problems before you develop full-blown symptoms, which are much harder to resolve. So if you spend many hours at a desk or you're elderly, start doing the following stretches now, as a preventive. Not only will you avoid future problems, you'll also improve your overall quality of life.

Office Worker

Even if you have no symptoms, as long as you have that office job, you're susceptible to developing a sunken chest, tight biceps, rounded shoulders, a compressed lower back, and short hip flexors. This program prevents or reverses these changes.

> Dead Roach 1 (page 90) → Dead Roach 2 (page 93)
> Steeple (page 96) → Holding a Small Globe (page 98)
> Side-of-Neck Stretch (page 115) → Shrug Muscle Stretch (page 122)
> Chest Muscle Stretch (page 127) → Broad Back Stretch (page 125)

> Front-of-Shoulder Stretch (page 117) → Biceps Stretch (page 129)
> Hip Flexor Stretch (page 136) → Human Pinwheel (page 145) →
> Hamstring Spectrum (page 157)

Elderly Person

This series of stretches targets all elderly people with no symptoms. The stretches preserve flexibility in your shoulders and keep your legs working well. If you've developed a moderate hump in your back, this program prevents it from progressing.

If you can't get down on the floor, here's how to adapt the stretches:

> Dead Roach 1 can be done in bed, which is great, since you go straight to sleep afterward.
> Do Holding a Small Globe in a chair with your feet flat on the floor, just pushing your arms up while pushing your feet into the floor.
> Hip Flexor Stretch is difficult, but I can't overemphasize its importance to an elderly person, since it straightens the spine and extends the hip. Do the easy version using two chairs if you need to (see page 138).

The Low Back Stretch must be done on the floor. Try your best to use the wall and a chair to lower yourself onto the floor. But if you can't, leave this stretch out.

If you can get on the floor but doing the Low Back Stretch with your arms overhead is too strenuous, for the first week keep your head on the floor and your hands on your abdomen while you work on moving your sacrum toward the floor and your heels toward the ceiling. Then add the overhead arms and the chin-tuck head position.

> Dead Roach 1 (page 90)
> Steeple (page 96) → Holding a Small Globe (page 98)
> Low Back Stretch (page 104)
> Biceps Stretch (page 129)
> Buttocks Muscle Stretch (page 143)
> Hip Flexor Stretch (page 136)

Healthy Person

Here are the spinal and fascial stretches *everyone* should do as a preventive three times a week. Fascial restrictions are constantly forming and so must be constantly released. This program keeps your head erect, minimizes rounding of the spine, decompresses the lower back, releases the hip flexor muscles, and keeps the hips nice and loose.

> ❯ Dead Roach 1 (page 90) → Dead Roach 2 (page 93)
> ❯ Steeple (page 96) → Holding a Small Globe (page 98)
> ❯ Low Back Stretch (page 104)
> ❯ Chest Muscle Stretch (page 127) → Biceps Stretch (page 129)
> ❯ Hip Flexor Stretch (page 136) → Hamstring Spectrum (page 157)
> ❯ Human Pinwheel (page 145) → Buttocks Muscle Stretch (page 143)

Note: if you don't have pain or restricted movement, this program won't create dramatic changes. However, you will begin to feel more comfortable in your body, and because of this your overall functioning—not just physical but also mental—will improve.

This program is great to do after long car and plane rides, and especially after workouts. You feel young, as though everything in your body is flowing and connected.

Additional Therapies to Boost Your Results

H ere's a collection of useful self-therapy techniques and tools, plus suggestions for several supplementary therapeutic treatments, all of which support the Ming Method and enhance your overall results. The self-therapy techniques help you do the fascial stretches more easily or assist in relieving pain. You can add them in as early as the preparatory phase of the program. The therapeutic treatments make the fascial stretches easier and support your body, especially during the most intensive phase of the strengthening program.

Hamstring Release

If you have difficulty with the Low Back Stretch and the Hamstring Spectrum, this release makes them easier.

Sit on a table or countertop that's high enough so your feet don't touch the floor. Put a tennis ball under your thigh, just 1 inch above the point where the knee bends. Lean back on your hands (see Figure 10-1). Use your buttocks muscles to exert moderate pressure down into the table (i.e., into the hamstrings). Point your toe and slowly straighten the leg, while continuing to press the thigh down.

If you're thin and light, press down gently on your thigh with the same-side hand, about 1 inch above the kneecap, to increase the pressure.

FIGURE 10-1

When your leg is fully extended, bend the toes back toward you (see Figure 10-2). Keeping the knee straight, lean forward slowly, maintaining the pressure on the back of the thigh (see Figure 10-3). Tense the front of the thigh. Hold this position for a couple of seconds; then repeat the entire procedure twice more.

Move the ball 1 inch up the back of your thigh, and repeat the foot raise and hold three times. Continue moving the ball up the thigh 1 inch at a time, repeating the procedure three times at each point, until the ball reaches your buttocks.

You can use this technique diagnostically. As you move the ball up the thigh, you'll find certain areas that are tender. Do five of the raise-and-holds at these points. Once you've found these spots, you can work just them instead of the entire thigh.

FIGURE 10-2

FIGURE 10-3

Sole-of-Foot Release

Use this technique for plantar fasciitis and Morton's neuroma. It also improves balance and is great for ballet dancers, runners, and basketball players.

You need to use a few drops of oil. I like castor oil, because it's not slippery and provides a bit of traction. Almond or coconut oil is also fine, but don't use mineral oil—it's petroleum based, is potentially toxic, and may clog your pores. Take your shoes and socks off, and rub just a tiny amount of oil on the sole of one foot and on the knuckles of the opposite hand.

Sit in a chair, and cross one foot over the other thigh so you can reach it. Keep the foot in neutral position—don't bend the ankle. Relax the foot, and hold the back of it with the same-side hand. Make a fist with the opposite hand, and place its knuckles on the ball of the foot.

Don't use the knuckles that connect the fingers to the hand; use the knuckles that connect the two longer segments of the fingers.

Use the same-side hand to apply some counterpressure to the back of the foot to keep it stable. Clench the toes as hard as you can (see Figure 10-4).

If you have trouble clenching the toes, practice bending them forward.

Dig the knuckles into the ball of the foot, using moderate pressure. Then rotate them downward toward the heel. Open your toes, and drag the knuckles down the foot 1 inch. Clench the toes again, dig the knuckles in at the point where they are, open the toes, and drag down another inch (see Figure 10-5). Repeat this action until you feel the heel bone; then continue ½ inch beyond it.

Be careful not to dig directly into a tendon with your knuckles. You know when you've done this because it hurts a lot. Try to slip the knuckles in between the tendons, which feel like hard cords under the skin of the sole.

You'll find quite a few hot, tender spots in your feet. Use less pressure at these points. After two or three treatments, these hot spots will dissolve.

 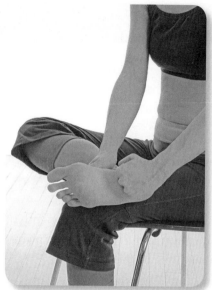

FIGURE 10-4   **FIGURE 10-5**

Caution: if you push too hard into your soles, you can injure yourself. So for the first three treatments, use only moderate pressure and increase it slowly, according to the Kaizen principle. Don't overdo: an entire treatment should take no longer than ninety seconds per foot.

IT Band Release

This technique releases the tight fascia (IT band) that runs down the outside of the thigh. It's good for relieving knee pain, hip pain, and lower-back pain.

You need a prop to roll on. The best type is a foam roller. Use one that's not too hard, or the treatment will be painful. If you don't have a roller, try a tightly rolled towel. Roll a large towel up tight, and tape around it to keep it well packed.

Lie on your side on the floor with the roller under the outside of your thigh just below the hip joint. Keep your bottom leg straight, cross the top leg over it, and place the top foot on the floor in front of you (see Figure 10-6).

Roll down the thigh about 5 inches, then roll up to the starting point, back and forth, until you find a hot (tender) spot. Stay on that spot, and straighten the bottom leg slowly and completely; then hold for one second. Now bend the bottom knee slowly and fully, and hold for one second (see Figure 10-7). Repeat this straighten-and-bend three times. Then roll back and forth three times, continuing to bend and straighten as you roll.

You don't need to bend and straighten according to any specific rhythm. Find the place where it hurts, roll up and down, and then bend and straighten a few times.

Starting at the bottom of the previous 5-inch segment that you rolled, roll down another 5 inches and repeat the previous procedure—finding a hot spot, straightening and bending the knee, and rolling as before.

Like the Hamstring Release, this technique is diagnostic as well as therapeutic. You'll find at least one, and possibly two, sensitive spots on the IT band to work on.

Caution: *do not overuse this technique, or you can wind up very sore and create even more inflammation. The entire treatment should last no longer than two minutes on a side.*

FIGURE 10-6

FIGURE 10-7

Palm Release

The Palm Release is excellent for typists, massage therapists, manual physical therapists, and others who work with their hands. It resembles the foot release.

Spread about three drops of oil over one palm. Place that hand palm up against your thigh near the knee, with the fingers extending down the inside of the thigh. Make a fist with the other hand, and dig the knuckles into the webbing between the fingers of the first hand. Clench the fingers of the first hand over those knuckles (see Figure 10-8).

Roll the knuckles into the palm, and open the clenched fingers as you drag the knuckles about 1 inch down the palm. Move farther down the palm, and repeat this action (see Figure 10-9).

Since the knuckles of the forefinger and middle finger are the powerful ones, you need to make several passes across the palm, as well as down it, so you can use these knuckles on the entire surface. Work down one side, the center, and then the other side. You should be able to work the entire hand with about ten passes.

Again, don't overdo it; the treatment should take no longer than ninety seconds per hand.

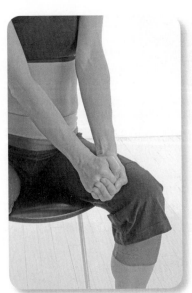

FIGURE 10-8

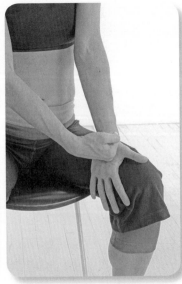

FIGURE 10-9

Quadriceps Release

This technique helps relieve knee, hip, and lower-back pain. It's good for runners and ballplayers.

You can do the Quadriceps Release on bare skin or through clothing. If you do it on bare skin, use a tiny bit of oil on the tip of your elbow, but make sure it's not slippery. You need traction.

Sit on a surface that's high enough that your feet don't touch the floor. Straighten your leg, and bend the toes back toward you. Holding your forearm horizontally in front of you, dig the same-side elbow into the top of your thigh, just above the kneecap. With your other hand, press the elbow down into the thigh (see Figure 10-10). Bend your knee, and as the leg moves backward, drag your elbow about 4 inches toward your hip, using moderate downward pressure (see Figure 10-11).

FIGURE 10-10

FIGURE 10-11

Straighten your leg again, and this time start the elbow 2 inches from the knee (you're overlapping half of the area you just worked) and drag another 4 inches. Repeat this procedure until the end of the last dragging movement reaches the hip. (For most people, this means three or four repeats.)

Ideally, sit right at the corner of a counter or table so you can bring the bent knee farther back than the front edge of the surface you're sitting on (as in Figure 10-11).

Since the thigh is quite wide, you need to do the entire procedure three times to find all the hot spots: first down the center and then down each side.

***Caution:** the point here is to drag the elbow; do not press down. Don't use so much downward force that it's painful; the pressure is just an aid to make the dragging effective.*

Side-of-Neck Release

This technique releases the scalenes, the same muscles affected by the Side-of-Neck Stretch. It's a key release for carpal tunnel syndrome, as well as for shoulder problems, tennis and golfer's elbow, and problems of the fingers, hands, and wrists.

Tilt your head to the right. Place the flat, straight fingers of your left hand underneath and slightly behind your right ear (see Figure 10-12). Now tilt your head to the left, and as the head moves, let the fingers slide down the side of the neck, pressing lightly as they move across your skin (see Figure 10-13). Slide the fingers until they touch your collarbone.

Do this twice more, starting at a point 1 inch forward of the previous point each time. On the third pass, you should end up at the inner end of your collarbone.

A dense complex of nerves underneath this area of the neck supplies the arm. The purpose of this release is to break up scar tissue that glues the scalenes to these nerves, thereby improving the nerves' function.

Caution: *these paper-thin muscles must be treated very gently. Your goal is to create just a slight amount of tension to begin breaking up the scar tissue. Do not do this treatment for more than a total of nine strokes per side (three strokes in each position). The entire treatment should take no more than forty-five seconds on each side. If you do it for longer than that, you risk irritating the area and creating an inflammation.*

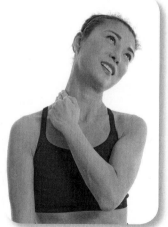

FIGURE 10-12   **FIGURE 10-13**

Sauna

I love a sauna after a workout, and I encourage you to take one whenever you can. The sauna promotes the flow of fluid within the fascia by opening up the tiny arteries—essential for the healing process—and it makes your tissue very supple. It enhances recuperation after a workout or stretch session and helps the body detoxify. Finally, because it's dry heat (unlike a steam room), it exercises the sweat glands so they work more efficiently.

Make sure you drink at least a pint of water before getting into the sauna. If you're not used to saunas, don't stay in longer than eight minutes the first time, and work gradually up to twenty minutes. **Caution:** if you have a heart problem or high blood pressure, consult a doctor first to make sure the sauna is safe for you. Be aware, too, that saunas can exacerbate skin disorders.

Traumeel and Zeel

Traumeel and Zeel are pain-relieving products with no known side effects, made by a German company called Heel. I find Traumeel really effective for myofascial aches and pains. It comes as an ointment or gel and is easy to find in health food stores, online, and even in some pharmacies. To get results you must use it three times a day for a week, rubbing it in deeply. Traumeel won't work if you just smooth it on; imagine you're pressing it deeply into your skin and keep massaging until it's completely gone and the skin is no longer slippery. Within an hour you should feel dramatic relief.

Zeel is a newer product made specifically for joint pain and arthritis. (When massaging it into the knee, make sure you don't press directly down onto the kneecap.) Since it's not yet widely known, you may find it only online.

Epsom Salt and Baking Soda Bath

This old-fashioned treatment is a powerful remedy for overall myofascial pain, and it detoxes your body as well. Use it especially for hip, knee, foot, and lower-back pain (it's harder to keep your shoulders submerged). A salt bath is a great way to start my program if you have fibromyalgia, lower-back pain, arthritic knees, ankle pain, or foot neuromas.

Add 2 cups of Epsom salt and 1 cup of baking soda to very hot water. Drink a pint of water half an hour before getting into the bath. Then start by soaking for only ten minutes and work up gradually to twenty to thirty minutes.

Rethinking Ice: A Contrarian View

I've added ice to this list primarily to tell you *not* to use it most of the time. In my opinion, ice is greatly overused—to the point where it limits the body's ability to heal.

Do not ice on a regular basis. Icing is primarily for acute injuries. If you have chronic pain, the only time icing is appropriate is when there's an acute exacerbation—say you stepped off the bus wrong and sprained your already painful knee so badly that it swelled up. Here you have a new problem superimposed on a chronic one, and icing is OK, as long as you do it within twenty-four hours of the incident. Never apply ice later than twenty-four hours after an injury. If you haven't iced it by then, don't ice it at all, since the reactions that occur at this point actually impair healing.

Here's how to ice properly: fifteen minutes on, applying light pressure with an Ace bandage or your hand, and then fifteen minutes off. Do this three times, the sooner after the injury the better—and that's it. Never put ice directly on your skin: use an ice pack or wrap it in a towel, and check periodically to make sure it's not sticking to your skin—otherwise you'll get frostbite.

An additional tip from my own experience: take enzymes before you ice. They increase the anti-inflammatory response, so you get much better results when you combine them with ice. Use about a third more than your regular dose, and take these extra enzymes on the day you ice and for one to two days afterward, until the inflammation subsides. You'll see a dramatic decrease in the swelling and pain.

Deep Tissue Massage

Deep tissue massage goes by various names. Therapists may say they do sports massage, deep friction massage, deep tissue massage, or just call themselves massage therapists. You want someone who can work deeply into the fascia and release adhesions. Try different practitioners until you find someone who can break up tough scar tissue. You can tell when this is happening, because scar tissue has a gristlelike quality that you can feel while the therapist is working on it. You also hear little crunches inside your tissue.

Related to deep tissue massage is Active Release Techniques (ART), a highly refined and sophisticated form of therapy in which the patient participates by moving a specific limb during the treatment. ART is now widespread, with practitioners available in most areas. Many chiropractors, physical therapists, and osteopaths now practice ART. Use the preceding criteria to make sure you've found an experienced therapist.

Another technique I particularly recommend is Rolfing (named after Dr. Ida Rolf, who developed it), which specifically targets the fascia. Rolfers receive rigorous training and as a result really understand fascia. Some Rolfers practice this work in a way that may cause more discomfort for the client than regular massage. Thus I suggest you look for Rolfers who work in a softer manner.

I also like Chinese Tui Na massage, which is similar to shiatsu or acupressure. It's based on a tried and tested four-thousand-year-old technique that goes hand-in-hand with myofascial stretching and acupuncture. Tui Na is growing increasingly popular, and practitioners are available all over the country at reasonable prices.

Getting deep tissue massages while doing the fascial program helps break up scar tissue and restores your fascia to a healthy gel-like state, facilitating the effects of the stretches and bringing more relief to painful hot spots and trigger points. Tip: half an hour before a massage, drink a pint of water to hydrate your tissue and take your highest dose of enzymes *or* joint support supplements (*not* both). If you can afford it, I recommend an hour-long massage every two weeks for the rest of your life.

Chiropractic and Osteopathy

The great value of chiropractic is that it adjusts the bones, which fascial stretching generally doesn't do. Bones out of place diminish the signals in nearby nerves, and a chiropractic treatment restores nerve function by realigning the bones. Thus I recommend an occasional chiropractic treatment.

The more conservative "straight" chiropractors focus strictly on bones, whereas more modern, holistic chiropractors include a variety of other healing methods in their practice. Be aware that to benefit from an adjustment you must be well hydrated, with your fascia at least partially released. *Do not* have a chiropractic treatment until you've completed the preparatory phase and have been stretching for at least two weeks.

Osteopaths are medical physicians who practice a wide range of conventional and alternative treatments, including a form of manual therapy that works well with fascial stretches. If you feel more comfortable consulting a practitioner who has a medical degree while also understanding complementary medicine, you may want to look for an osteopath.

Acupuncture

Acupuncture, another ancient therapy, enhances the Ming Method by opening up the flow of energy through the body so that healing processes can occur more effectively. Some experts believe that this energy actually flows through the network of fascia, allowing all parts of the body to communicate. A bonus: acupuncturists use traditional Chinese diagnostic techniques, including examining your tongue and taking several pulses, which gives you useful additional information about your body as a whole.

Many acupuncturists also offer traditional Chinese treatments called Gua Sha and cupping (which I practice myself). In Gua Sha, the skin is scraped with a special implement. In cupping, the practitioner creates a vacuum under glass cups placed on the skin. Both techniques are traditionally performed to improve energy flow, but I recommend them because they also increase the flow of fluid through the fascia and help unkink it.

Treatments on the Cutting Edge

Last, I want to introduce you to two supplemental therapies that I use in my practice. Although relatively new and somewhat esoteric, they're rapidly gaining acceptance. If you can't find a practitioner near you now, no doubt you'll be able to shortly.

These therapies are part of what is known as energy medicine, which involves the idea that the body is not only a physical system but an energy system as well. Your cell phone or microwave works by emitting energy waves at specific frequencies. In the same way, the body has its own energy frequencies, which have been measured scientifically. The use of energy to heal body problems is the basis of quite a few healing modalities, including Therapeutic Touch, acupuncture, and qigong. Energy medicine treatments promote healing by changing the electromagnetic frequency of injured tissue to that of normal tissue. The field of energy medicine has attracted much interest, and the National Center for Complementary and Alternative Medicine, part of the National Institutes of Health, funds research on various forms of energy healing.

The two following energy treatments are best administered by a professional. (Although self-treatment versions of these technologies are available, to be truly effective these methods require the expertise of a professional trained to administer them.) I prefer cold laser, which doesn't require attaching electrodes to the body and takes less time. However, both modalities give essentially the same results. I recommend them because in addition to release of the fascia, getting your body to its most optimal level requires making sure that its energy system is fully functional. So consider one of these treatments after you've completed the preparatory program plus two weeks of stretching (the treatments also facilitate both stretching and strength training). If you can find a medical practitioner well versed in either microcurrent or cold laser, you'll be in great shape.

Microcurrent

Microcurrent is a form of physical therapy that applies an extremely low level of electrical current to injured areas of the body. It's painless and totally different from the standard electrostimulation and ultrasound treatments used by many physical therapists, which deliver much higher frequencies. Supporters of microcurrent believe that the standard treatments are too strong for the cells and may harm them. In my own experience, standard electrostimulation or ultrasound (which converts sound waves into heat) temporarily relieves symptoms, but never solves the underlying problem.

Microcurrent's effect is based on the theory that all the cells in your body can talk to one another. Research indicates that each cell has its own signature electromagnetic frequency, and that cells communicate with each other via these frequencies, bypassing the nervous system. If you drop a pebble into a pond, the water ripples outward in waves to every part of the pond. If you get hit in the stomach, every part of your body feels the injury in some way via ripples of electromagnetic energy. It's believed that our capacity for precise, rapid movement actually depends on this energy-wave communication system working with the nervous system.

According to the theory, optimal healing requires that the energetic communication system be intact. Kinked fascia represents an interruption of communication—a roadblock that stops the flow of information. This is why surgery should always be your very last resort: it actually creates those roadblocks by cutting through the fascia. Microcurrent is believed to promote healing by changing the frequency of damaged cells to that of normal healthy cells, thereby restoring their ability to communicate. The practitioner sets specific frequencies on the microcurrent apparatus according to the type of tissue being healed.

As I see it, microcurrent speaks the language of cells in a soft way that they can understand—I think of it as whispering to the cells. When I use it on my patients, it dramatically softens kinked fascia, increases blood flow, and reduces swelling, inflammation, and spasm, relieving pain and initiating a healing process that helps resolve the underlying problem. It also strengthens muscles. Most people need treatments lasting fifteen minutes to an hour, twice a week for a couple of weeks.

Cold Laser

Also called low-level laser therapy, cold laser uses a laser beam that produces no heat at all. Laser works in a way similar to microcurrent: it changes the frequency of injured cells so that energy can flow through them. Shining the laser light onto a painful area significantly decreases pain and swelling and increases joint flexibility. Lasering the pathway of a nerve that isn't working stimulates the nerve to start firing again. In most cases, immediately after the treatment, the muscle supplied by that nerve is dramatically stronger.

I give all my patients a laser treatment at the end of their session, and it makes a huge difference: painful swellings go down, and they immediately become stronger and more flexible, right in front of my eyes. Many companies now make these devices; the one I prefer is the Erchonia.

Sleep!

A very underestimated aspect of healing is getting enough sleep. During sleep, your body releases a cascade of hormones that promote recuperation. Sleep also reduces levels of cortisol, a hormone related to stress. You simply can't negotiate your sleep: it has to be done right, no less than eating does. No matter what your pain problem, you will not heal completely without enough sleep. The bonus: a healthy sleep pattern decreases sugar cravings, and a lower intake of sugar prevents inflammation.

I suggest going to sleep before 11 P.M. Do not watch TV or do any stimulating activity for at least two hours before bedtime. Make sure your room is cool (since the body sleeps better in cooler temperatures) and as dark as possible. Eliminate as much ambient light as you can: block light from windows, cover the LED display on your clock radio, or use an eyeshade. You want to have the room as close to pitch-dark as you can get, since light blocks the release of melatonin, an important sleep-promoting hormone.

Try to get a minimum of eight and a half hours of sleep a night. I'm also a firm believer in the benefits of napping. If you can manage it, a half-hour nap between 1:00 and 4:00 in the afternoon reboots your system and gives your body extra support to heal. (Some companies now recognize that napping during work breaks increases productivity.) I urge you to take your sleep as seriously as you do your water drinking. Like water, sleep is the cheapest possible medicine.

As I explained in Chapter 3, I believe that using just one therapy to heal a body problem is not nearly so effective as using many. That's why I'm happy to beg, borrow, and steal from a wide range of healing modalities. No one knows everything, and there are weaknesses in every system—including mine. No single system will cure you.

In line with my philosophy of empowering you to take charge of your own healing, this chapter has offered a variety of extra tools for doing just that. It's your role to weigh them, see what makes sense, give those measures an honest try, and come up with a system that's well balanced, well researched, and works for you. I believe that if you follow my program and add in some of the techniques and therapies in this chapter, you'll have created a truly complete healing program—and will spare yourself many unnecessary medications, possibly unnecessary surgery, and a whole lot of misery.

Index